Andrew S. Cahan

4880 Lower Valley Road, Atglen, PA 19310 USA

Dedication

For Debbie

Published by Schiffer Publishing Ltd.
4880 Lower Valley Road
Atglen, PA 19310
Phone: (610) 593-1777; Fax: (610) 593-2002
E-mail: Info@schifferbooks.com

For the largest selection of fine reference books on this and related subjects, please visit our web site at **www.schifferbooks.com**
We are always looking for people to write books on new and related subjects. If you have an idea for a book please contact us at the above address.

This book may be purchased from the publisher.
Include $3.95 for shipping.
Please try your bookstore first.
You may write for a free catalog.

In Europe, Schiffer books are distributed by
Bushwood Books
6 Marksbury Ave.
Kew Gardens
Surrey TW9 4JF England
Phone: 44 (0) 20 8392-8585; Fax: 44 (0) 20 8392-9876
E-mail: info@bushwoodbooks.co.uk
Free postage in the U.K., Europe; air mail at cost.

Library of Congress Cataloging-in-Publication Data

Cahan, Andrew S.
  Chinese label art, 1900-1976 / Andrew S. Cahan.
    p. cm.
  ISBN 0-7643-2379-2 (pbk.)
  1. Labels—China—Themes, motives 2. Commercial art—China—History—20th century. I. Title.
  NC1002.L3C35 2006
  741.6'9209510904—dc22

                    2005035054

Copyright © 2006 by Andrew S. Cahan

    All rights reserved. No part of this work may be reproduced or used in any form or by any means—graphic, electronic, or mechanical, including photocopying or information storage and retrieval systems—without written permission from the publisher.
    The scanning, uploading and distribution of this book or any part thereof via the Internet or via any other means without the permission of the publisher is illegal and punishable by law. Please purchase only authorized editions and do not participate in or encourage the electronic piracy of copyrighted materials.
    "Schiffer," "Schiffer Publishing Ltd. & Design," and the "Design of pen and ink well" are registered trademarks of Schiffer Publishing Ltd.

Cover and book designed by: Bruce Waters
Type set in ZapfHumanist Demi BT/Benguiat Bk

ISBN: 0-7643-2379-2
Printed in China

Contents

Introduction ------ 4

Chapter 1. Early Chinese Label Art ------ 7

Chapter 2. Religion, Symbolism, and the Supernatural ------ 24

Chapter 3. Westernization and Modernity ------ 58

Chapter 4. Art Deco ------ 68

Chapter 5. Women in Chinese Advertising ------ 80

Chapter 6. Children in Chinese Advertising ------ 100

Chapter 7. The Animal Kingdom ------ 110

Chapter 8. Transportation ------ 122

Chapter 9. Patriotism and the Military ------ 132

Chapter 10. The People's Republic of China, 1949-1976 ------ 146

Bibliography and Suggested Reading ------ 159

Credits ------ 160

Note: Several phonetic systems are used in this book. Where a Chinese word is spelled phonetically in English on a label, I have retained the original spelling used. Otherwise, for words pertaining to items made outside of mainland China, or in pre-1949 mainland China, the Wade-Giles system is used. For items made in post-1949 mainland China, the pinyin system is used.

Acknowledgements

The author would like to thank the following people for their help, inspiration, and encouragement:

Debbie Simmons-Cahan
Suzy Cahan
Suyu and Edward Martinique
Lino Nivolo
Katie Riggsbee
Sam Wai Lon
Andrew Robert Cahan
Robert Schoonhoven

And last but definitely not least, my mother, Elaine Brownstein, for her love, encouragement, and my childhood excursions to Chinatown and the Far East.

Introduction

My first exposure to Chinese culture occurred in 1959, during the lunar new-year celebration in New York City's Chinatown. Never before had I seen anything like the colorful, noisy, boisterous scene that was taking place. I was but a year old. But somehow, the experience seems to have given rise to a lifelong fascination with all things Chinese.

Throughout childhood, my greatest thrill was to walk around Chinatown, in the old Five Points area, in lower Manhattan. I would peruse shops full of exotic products from the land on the other side of the world. Store owners were often perplexed by this non-Chinese boy who would spend hours looking through incense, medicines, teas, canned foods, and traditional almanacs, buy a Chinese newspaper, and take a souvenir business card before leaving.

At a certain point, my interest in China caused my parents to wonder whether, at the age of ten, I might actually have an FBI file. I loved listening to short wave radio, especially when conditions were favorable for picking up stations from Asia. Sometime in the late 1960s, during the middle of the Cultural Revolution, I wrote to Radio Peking for a listener's confirmation (QSL) card. I received a warm letter from the station with the card. After about a month passed, I began receiving parcels of propaganda publications from the People's Republic of China. The packages continued to come on a regular basis for about five years.

Other childhood contact with the region consisted of years of correspondence with pen pals in Hong Kong and Macau. At around the age of thirteen, I submitted my name to the pen pal list in Hong Kong's *South China Morning Post*. I had found the paper in the crumpled remains of packing material from a discarded box in an Asian gift shop. My listing yielded about one hundred responses from children in Hong Kong and Macau, some of whom I corresponded with for years.

At fifteen, I finally had the opportunity to travel to this wondrous region, and spent time in Hong Kong, Macau, and Taipei. The tourist sights were interesting, but my best adventure was exploring the old shops, where the merchants eyed me with even more puzzlement than in Chinatown. Having traveled back to the area several times as an adult, I have become used to the perplexed looks I still get while gathering up seemingly incongruous merchandise that Westerners usually don't take interest in. Fortunately, a few collectibles dealers in Asia have taken notice of the growing interest in remnants of China's past popular cultures. Items once regarded as junk are viewed as treasures of graphic beauty and interest, at least to the small handful of enthusiasts from around the world.

But, back to the 1960s.

Ironically, Independence Day in the United States provided a fine opportunity to collect advertising art from Asia. Every 4th and 5th of July, I'd bike through the neighborhoods, searching the streets for remnants of paper left by spent firecracker

Advertisement for traditional Chinese face reading, printed in the May 3, 1955 issue of *The Chinese Journal*, a newspaper published in New York City's Chinatown.

packs. At that time, fireworks were imported to the U.S. mainly from Macau, a small Portuguese territory on the South China coast. If it was a really lucky day, I would find an intact pack label. Each new find rewarded me with a view into another small fantasy world brimming with color, mystery, and beauty. In many cases, I couldn't quite interpret what I was looking at, but that only made these items more intriguing. Brands and images often seemed to have little to do with firecrackers at all. And there was the Chinese writing—unintelligible to me, but mesmerizing to look at and to imagine the meanings. All of this added a mystical aura to an extraordinary product. (Firecracker labels continue to be my favorite collectibles, and, as the reader may notice, they figure prominently in the selection for this book.)

Soon I discovered that those curious designs and scenes were not limited to fireworks labels, but adorned many other Chinese products. The graphics on packages of incense, teas, foods, medicines, and many other products were abundant with symbolism and visual excitement. The old designs captured my interest the most.

Around 1973, a radical change began to transpire in the look of firecracker labels and other packaging from China. The ornate and complex designs with mythological scenes, animals, children, and cartoon-like imagery were suddenly being replaced by stark, serious, and literal depictions of things like radio towers, bridges, and buildings. I couldn't quite make the connection at first, but the changes were the result of the re-opening of trade and diplomatic relations between the U.S. and the People's Republic of China (PRC).

The artwork I had reveled in had actually been produced not in mainland China, but in places such as Macau, Hong Kong, Taiwan, and Singapore, places largely populated by Chinese people, but not under the governmental jurisdiction of mainland China. It was in these areas that the more traditional Chinese designs and aesthetics were able to continue thriving after the 1949 Communist revolution, and for decades after. The designs produced within communist China had long since begun the transformation to government regulated forms that reflected political circumstances surrounding life in post-revolutionary communist China.

The thawing condition of U.S.-China trade relations in the 1970s accelerated the disappearance of older themes and styles. Manufacture and export firms located outside of the PRC had previously dominated manufacture and export of Chinese products to the U.S. during the embargo that had begun in the U.S. in December 1950. When trade relations between the U.S. and China began to resume, many of these firms began their financial descent, due to the cheap labor in the PRC. With the folding of those businesses, much of the older design aesthetics of labeling and packaging also met their demise.

The imagery and decoration used on labels, packages, and posters often reflected the nature of the times and places in which they were produced. The evolution of twentieth century Chinese advertising was shaped by changes in politics, technology, and levels of foreign contact.

Chinese branding and packaging drew design inspiration from sources such as folk beliefs and religion, the social and political climate, current and historical events, and other realms of popular consciousness. To those unfamiliar with Chinese labeling, a brand or design may sometimes seem to have little relation to the product itself—it is likely that the design was chosen instead for its ability to stir positive associations within the potential consumer. Products were marketed under brands and trademarks with themes as diverse as fashionable women, Buddhist deities, symbolic animals, wealth, spousal loyalty, automobiles, political parties, architecture, sex, fashion, youth, age, and so on.

Presented in this book is a selection of some of the most interesting and beautiful items I have found over the years. They are from products made for both the domestic Chinese market as well as for export. Most were obtained while exploring Chinatowns on the East Coast, on numerous trips to Macau and Hong Kong, at flea markets, antique shops, auctions, and through fellow collectors. Difficult as it is to find such things, it is still possible to discover remnants of old world Chinese products and packaging that somehow survived to the present. Much of this material is comprised of forgotten ephemera and objects that were accidentally saved; some items had been left on the back shelves of tiny traditional shops or abandoned factories, for example. As China continues to reinvent itself, most of the remaining traditional shops are lingering through their last days, facing the likelihood of being replaced by a modern structure of little regional character at any time. When the historical and artistic significance of everyday things from the past is finally pondered, it is usually after much time and change have transpired, and remnants are all that remain.

Chapter 1

Early Chinese Label Art

For hundreds of years prior to the advent of lithography and other newer technologies in China, wood block printing shops were numerous, and in great demand. Books, New Year posters (nianhua), religious paper, and advertising labels had been manufactured using block-printing methods at least as far back as the Song Dynasty (A.D. 960-1279). Although lithography was introduced to China in the nineteenth century, wood block printing is still occasionally used even today to produce joss paper and a few other traditional products.

In old China, wood block printed New Year pictures of gods and auspicious images were displayed in homes and businesses during the lunar new-year celebration, and often throughout the year. These images of deities, mythological and legendary characters, and happy earthly situations were available not just to the affluent, but to ordinary people who used them as "functional art." The icons and scenes on these posters were familiar symbolic representations of wealth, health, and happiness, as well as scenes of celebration. The display of such images was thought to protect and bring well-being to the household and business. Nianhua drew upon, and helped to solidify the repertoire of images instilled in Chinese graphic art. The subjects and aesthetics of these decorative New Year images were quite influential on later Chinese commercial label and advertising design.

Etched bronze printing plates began to be used in China during the thirteenth century. The earliest surviving example, a block from the 1200s, was used to print labels for packages of sewing needles from Jinan Liu's Fine Needle Shop, in Shantung Province. The trademark was the traditional Chinese mythological motif of a white rabbit pounding a mortar and pestle. It is clearly depicted in the center, under a horizontal line of characters, and is flanked by a column of vertical characters on each side. There is an area for text below the trademark that is used to proclaim the attributes of the product and its maker. In addition, it suggests remembering the trademark in order to discern the best, as well as to avoid imitations. This format was commonly used on many product labels well into the first half of the twentieth century.

Popular prints and nianhua had a great deal of variety in their designs and functions. Colorful depictions of door-gods and the kitchen-god were displayed throughout the year for protection, while seasonal pictures were most often displayed during specific times of the year, at particular festivals and ceremonies.

Pictures honoring deities of agricultural and other specific work trades were created and used as channels between tradesmen and the beings in heaven who oversaw their efforts. Also produced in the old printing shops was paper joss, a general term for the myriad of religious paper burned or displayed to convey prayer and petition for specific needs. The wood blocks used to print joss paper tend to have been simply carved, and often depicted images that have become formalized through the centuries. Joss paper depicted charms, symbols, prayers, and images of deities, and was printed in mass quantities. Spirit money, loose imitations of paper bills, was a type of joss paper that was burned in order to send wealth to one's deceased ancestors. Symbolic representations of clothing and luxury items were printed, assembled, and then burned to send to the ancestors as gifts. This would ensure that the spirits' journey through the stages of hell would be more comfortable, and therefore encourage an ancestor's good grace.

Early printed labels were often no more than a red or neutral piece of paper with a simple block printing in gold or black ink, and similar in appearance to joss paper. The label carried the name of the product, the name of the shop or factory that produced it, and perhaps a small testimony pointing out the product's merits. Often, a brand or trademark was assigned. As illiteracy among the general Chinese population was widespread, it made good business sense to assign an easily recognizable illustration that consumers could associate with a particular brand. Brand loyalty could be fostered if a person could discern one maker from another by its package art. Manufacturers often pointed out that recognition of their trademark could enable the consumer to discern the genuine article from the imitations. Trademarks could also serve as product indicators for foreigners, who could not read the Chinese characters on exported items.

China's first lithographic printing shop was established in Shanghai, in 1876. By the early 1900s, many calendar and New Year posters were being lithographed, and by the 1920s, lithography was the primary method of printing commercial labels. For many firms, this meant production of their first color labels, and it was not uncommon for this to be announced in small print, at the top of these labels.

The visual aesthetics of the traditional block carvers and engravers continued to influence label designs long after lithography became the primary printing technique.

Wood block printed firecracker label. A border containing vases (symbolic of peace), a variety of plants, and a traditional angular, abstract maze-like motif surround the text. The consumer is given "suggestions for use," which tell some of the many traditional uses for firecrackers: the celebration of the birth of a son; the grand opening of a business; a wedding; hitting the jackpot, etc. Chung Cheng Kee Firecracker Factory, Macau, c.1900.

Carved wooden printing blocks. (left): Product label from Macau. (right): Block for printing traditional spirit money, adorned with symbols of happiness and prosperity. Macau, c. early to mid 1900s.

Wood block printed book cover. The border design includes a vase holding lotus flowers. Other features include a deer beside ling chih (the fungus of immortality); a phoenix or peacock; and bamboo, each with positive symbolic connotations. The three characters at the top are overlaid on three pomegranates, auspicious fruits associated with fertility and offspring. Canton, China, early 1900s.

Firecracker label. Best Golden Dragon Firecrackers. The border contains emblems associated with the legendary Eight Taoist Immortals. Choey Sun Firecracker Factory, Canton, China c. early 1900s.

Firecracker label. Wood block printed firecracker label depicting Victorian style images of Caucasian women, as well as a curious, elephant-like composite animal used as a trademark. Most likely made for export to the U.S. or England. Yuen Shing Firecracker Factory, Canton, China, c.1900.

Firecracker label. Cash (coin) trademark. Him San Fire-cracker Factory, Canton, China, c.1910s-20s.

Chinese incense made for religious use is often referred to as "joss sticks." Main centers of manufacture were Hong Kong, Macau, and Canton. Joss sticks were packed in bundles, and often sported elaborate pictures of gods, deities, and visions of paradise. The border of this example depicts the Eight Taoist Immortals below a pair of phoenixes. Chan Lun Hing Co., Macau and Kwangtung, c.1920s.

Block printed joss stick labels from companies in Canton, China, c.1920s.

Firecracker label. Cocks Crowing At the Sun Brand. Tung Cheong Firecracker Factory, Macau, early 1900s.

Tea packet wrapper. Trademark: flute-playing fairies riding phoenixes. Luen Chong Tai Co., Hong Kong, c.1920s.

Tea box label. Block-printed, using gold ink on red paper. Luen Chong Tai Co., Hong Kong, c.1910s-20s.

Firecracker box label. Lavish labels made from embossed, painted gold foil were created for use on fireworks boxes and crates from the mid nineteenth century until 1910. The subject of these labels centered around religious scenes, old legends, and various slices of Chinese life. Today they are commonly referred to as "Fat Shan labels," as most of the shops that manufactured these labels were located in the Fat Shan area of Canton. This particular example is a work of intricacy and detail created by a team of workers who performed different tasks as it was produced. Unlike most of the Fat Shan labels produced in the nineteenth century, the foil is not embossed, but is an intricate composite of gold foil, paint, colored paper, traditional paper cutting, and delicately painted imagery. The lack of embossing and the presence of colored background paper with a "shiny" finish may indicate a later manufacturing date, possibly the 1910s-20s. The foil frames the central image, and is cut in many places to expose a layer of orange paper behind it. Repeating patterns, symbolic fruits and flowers, and a butterfly with cash coin motif in each corner frame a delicately painted traditional Chinese scene on another layer of paper. This particular example shows a well-to-do elderly man and his attendants viewing a performance of traditional Chinese opera. All are dressed in Ching Dynasty clothing, detailed with finely brushed ornamental patterns in silver and gold ink. The central image is also finely cut in areas to enhance the design. This type of label is an expression of the importance placed on firecrackers, which in traditional Chinese culture had many religious and symbolic uses. Fat Shan, Canton, China, c. early 1900s-1920s.

Firecracker label. Early classic style engraving, with scenes from Chinese legends used as border decoration. Lion and ball trademark. House shaped borders such as this began use on property deeds, regional bank notes, medicine leaflets, and other documents of importance during the Ching Dynasty (1644-1911). The roof-shaped top symbolized security, value, wealth, and authenticity. It was later adopted for use on product labels, as a way of conveying similar associations to the consumer. Lee Yee Kee Co., China, c. early 1900s.

Incense label. Early, classic style label. China, c. early 1900s.

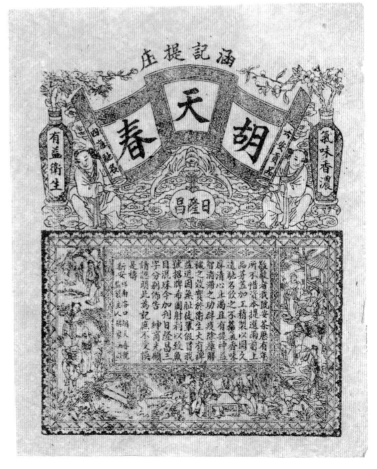

Firecracker label. The scene, with a happy and prosperous family under two dragons, bears strong influence from the New Year poster (nianhua) tradition. The panel at the bottom contains a Ki Lin, a highly benevolent mythological creature, surrounded by symbolic Buddhist objects. Chien Lung Hsiang Co., China, c. early 1900s.

Firecracker label or advertising poster. The label boasts of real value and honest price; of no deception of the elderly or youth; and a variety of quality firecrackers that are renowned throughout the world. Cheng Chung Hsing Co., China, c.1920.

Tea tin. Fabric covered oolong tea packaging. A lion and cash coins motif is used for the trademark. Hong Kong and Canton, China, c. early 1900s.

Firecracker label. Traditional basket fisherman. Kwong Hun Shing Co., Kwangtung, China, c.1920.

Candle labels. Best Unicorn Brand. Packaging on many of China's early export products included product and brand information in English. Often, the artist or letterer had to copy words onto the layout without necessarily having much knowledge of the English language. This pair of labels is one such example. Top: The striped Chinese flag was in use from 1912 through 1928. Bottom: The Nationalist Chinese Flag was adopted in 1928 and used on the mainland until 1949.

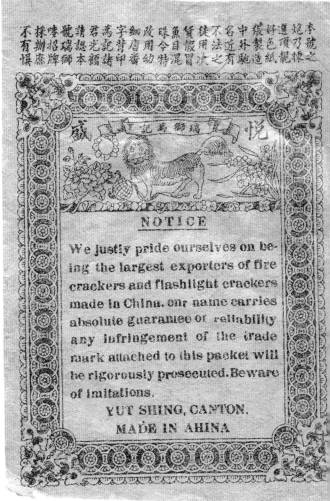

Firecracker labels. Two examples of labels printed within engraved "stock" or generic borders inspired by designs found on European and American paper money. The trademark is another example of the traditional and very popular lion with ball motif. The first of the two labels is the earlier, and bears a remarkable English translation of what is basically a "beware of imitation" message:

"We Have Spared Neither Pains Now Money Using Nest Paper and Can Power to Make Our Fire Crackers Which Set More Quickly is it and Give Aluder Sound Then Thost His Where and Have Become to Famous New in China and in Foreign Countries Neither Are So Me Un Proved Cuclar People Who imitate Our Trade Make Ploof Rememder But it is None Expect That Which Hears the Lithographs Lion Trade Mark."

This label caught the notice of Thomas Steep, who cited it in the chapter "Pidgin-English and Oriental Conversation" in his 1925 book entitled *Chinese Fantastics*. The second version of the label contains a revised version of the text. Yut Shing Co., Canton, China, 1920s.

Tea box. Flying Fairly (sic) & Two Phoenixes Facing the Sun Brand. Luen Chong Tai Tea Dealer, Hong Kong, c. 1920.

Firecracker label. The bow and arrow sometimes signified the arrival of a male baby, and was used in ceremonies to ward off evil spirits. The company name characters are displayed on three auspicious fruits: (left to right) the pomegranate (many children), peach (longevity), and the citron known as Buddha's Hand (wealth). A stylized bat hovers over the entire design, symbolizing happiness and longevity. Kwong Hing Lung Co., Macau, early 1900s.

Incense box. Chan Lun
Hing, Macau, c.1920.

Canned fruit label. Swatow Canning
Co., Swatow, China, c.1920s.

Tea packet with a seal of authenticity:
the proprietor's portrait. Tack Kee Co.,
Canton, China, c.1920.

Cigarette pack wrapper. Fisherman. Shantung Province, China, c.1930.

Tea tin. Ying Mee Co., Hong Kong, c.1920.

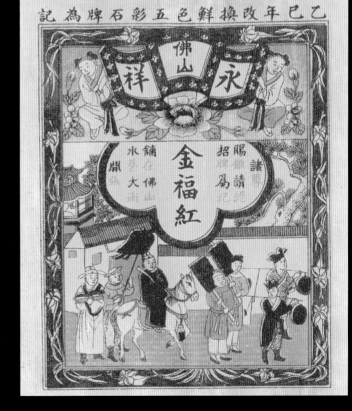

Firecracker label. Procession honoring a man who has done well on his civil examinations. Such exams were used until the fall of the Ching Dynasty in 1911, to select appropriate government officials. The signs carried indicate the tested man's great success. Wing Cheung Co., Fat Shan, Canton, China, early 1900s.

Firecracker label. A celebration of a high mark attained on the civil service examinations. The signs proclaim the highest rank of scholars who passed the imperial exams. Kwong Yuen Firecracker Factory, Macau and Canton, c. early 1900s.

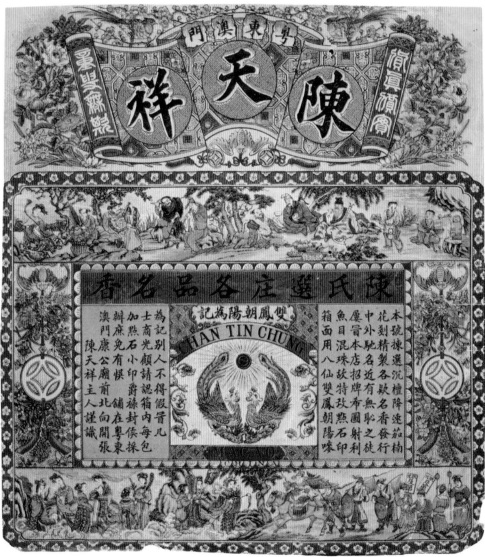

Joss sticks label. Fraught with detail and symbolism, this early incense label depicts deities, symbolic animals, flowers, and a procession (lower right) honoring a Ching dynasty scholar who achieved the highest rank in the civil examinations. The text proclaims the firm to give real value at an honest price, with no deception whether the customer is youthful or elderly. Chan Tin Chung Co., Macau and Kwangtung, c. early 1900s.

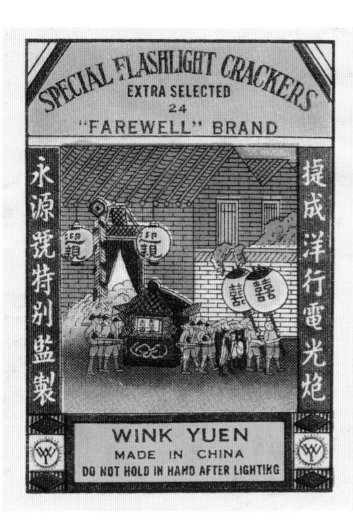

Firecracker labels. Farewell Brand.
Urban and rural scenes of wedding
processions. Wink Yuen Firecracker
Co., Canton, China, 1920s.

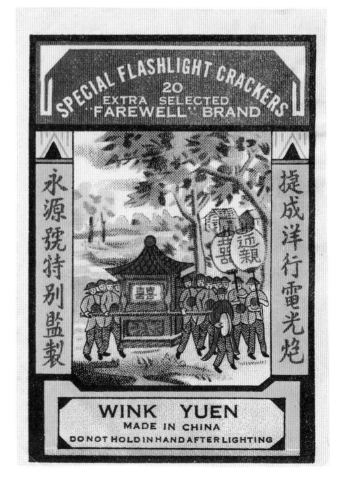

Firecracker label. Whoopee Brand. Traditional procession led
by Nationalist Chinese military men holding the national flag
adopted in 1928. Chen Cheong Co., China, c.1930s.

Firecracker label. Duck Brand. New Year celebration scene,
lion dance procession. Note the God of Longevity, Shou
Hsing, at right. Yick Loong Firecracker Co., Macau, c.1930.

Firecracker label. Happy Brand. Traditional celebration pastime: exploding firecrackers. Yau Wing Hong Co., China, c.1930s-40s.

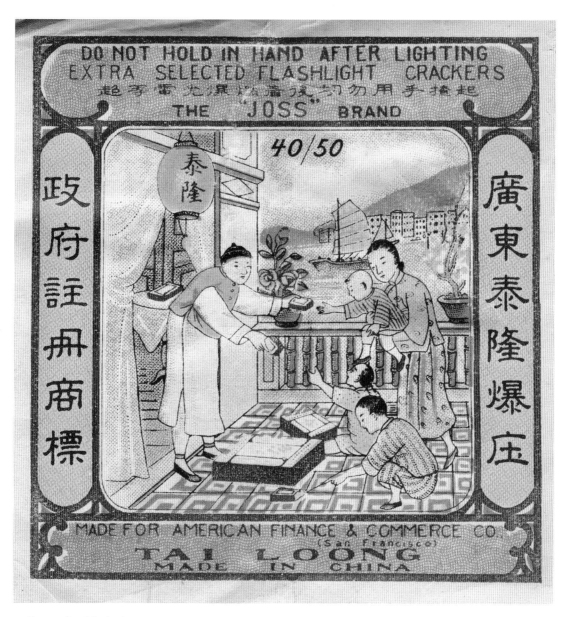

Firecracker label. The Joss Brand. Handing out money and firecrackers to children during the New Year celebration. Tai Loong Co., Canton, China, 1920s.

Chapter 2
Religion, Symbolism, and the Supernatural

In the Western world, religious symbols and sacred beings are seldom used to advertise and sell commercial products to the public. The practice is generally regarded as inappropriate—demeaning to the icon, and an affront those who regard it as sacred. As such, the practice would be bad for business as well.

Chinese tradition has regarded the issue in a different light. The rich pantheon of religious entities, mythological animals, and symbols that developed through the centuries contributed immensely to early commercial design. The implication was that good fortune could come from using a product associated with a positive religious symbol or a being that could bring good luck, good health, and prosperity. A trademark derived from the spiritual world associated the manufacturer with positive influences and financial success.

Traditional popular Chinese systems of faith evolved from an amalgam of influences from Buddhism, Taoism, Confucianism, ancient cult beliefs, and supernatural folklore. As in any tradition-based society, countless regional variations existed as well. Within the belief systems that evolved in China, the demarcation between the spirit world and the routine of daily life was not clearly delineated. In fact, the majority of Chinese deities had at one time been ordinary human beings who attained supernatural powers during their lifetimes, and at death became sacred beings in the spiritual realm. Yet communication with such beings was not out of the reach of the average mortal on Earth. Deities and ancestors had the power to affect people in all aspects of daily life. A show of respect through ritual and prayer was imperative, so as not to upset the harmony of the lives of those still earth-bound. Part of this worship involved the display of images of deities, gods, and ancestors. This was a common practice in most traditional Chinese households. In the commercial world, merchants and tradesmen used a wide variety of images of gods with specific protection capabilities or the ability to increase business. In a culture where visual images were important vehicles for worship, their use on packaging and labeling was an accepted application. Associating a potent religious icon with commercial product enhanced sales by tapping into the consumer's desire to become empowered by those in the spiritual realm.

Folk legends and mythological animals have been common motifs in Chinese art and decoration, and were important sources of ideas to label designers as well.

Mythological Animals

Dragon

The Dragon is the most auspicious and complex of the Chinese mythological menagerie. Thought of as good-natured and benign, yet extremely powerful, the dragon represents the yang, or male forces, and has a host of positive attributes and abilities.

Firecracker label. Best Golden Dragon Cannon Crackers. Kwong Kee Cheong, Canton, China, c.1910s-20s.

Record label. Columbia Phonograph Co., China, c.1910s-early 1920s.

Receipt letterhead. Two Dragons. The two-dragon motif represents the wish for rain. Hong Kong, c.1920s.

Merchandise wrapper. Sheung Chuk Chai Shoes Manufactory, Hong Kong, c.1930s.

Firecracker label. Best Double Dragon Lady Firecrackers. "Treasure Tripod" trademark—the ancient three-footed vessel was used by emperors in ritual ceremonies and eventually evolved into a symbol of good luck. Old Yuen Kee, Hong Kong, c.1930.

Firecracker label. Dragon. Made in China for the Australian market. Kwong Man Lung Firecracker Factory, Hong Kong, c.1930s-40s.

Firecracker label. Auspicious animals. A dragon, fish, and two phoenixes adorn this elaborate, embossed label. Wong Kwong Hing Ho Kee, Canton, China, 1926.

Firecracker label. Double Dragon Shooting Bead Brand. Dragons are often shown playing with, chasing, or vomiting a flaming pearl. Another version of this label gives the brand name as Double Dragon Disgorging Pearl. Sam Yick Sui Kee, Macau, c.1950.

Phoenix

The Phoenix is considered to be the highest ranking bird. It is among the most prominent of mythological creatures, and is thought to be composed of parts of several animals. These body parts are also thought to represent the five human qualities: head=virtue; wings=duty; back=correct behavior; breast=humanity; stomach=reliability. The phoenix appears only in times of peace and prosperity. It symbolizes good fortune, fertility, good harvest, longevity, and has many other positive attributes.

Firecracker label. Dragon and phoenix. When pictured together, the dragon and phoenix represent a newly wedded couple; the powerful union of a perfect yin/yang balance. Him Yuen Firecracker Factory, Macau, c.1950s.

Firecracker label. Phoenix and factories. The appearance of a phoenix in the midst of industrialization and modern technology. Nan Hai, People's Republic of China, c. late 1950s.

Ki Lin

The Ki Lin is an auspicious creature of purity, benevolence, and righteousness. It is said that a Ki Lin never brings harm to living thing, even to the point that it does not step on insects or damage plants as it walks. The Ki Lin never steals food, nor does it drink impure water. He is the chief of the hairy creatures, as man is thought to embody the essence of the naked creatures. As is the case with most other mythological Chinese creatures, the Ki Lin is composed of parts of several other animals. He is sometimes referred to, in English, as a unicorn, and is often shown with one horn. More often though, he has two or three.

A Ki Lin was said to appear only if the head of a state was running the government well, and had the support of the people. He is often depicted with a cloud-like image containing a scroll. This represents the belief that he appeared and spurted the Book of Law, when Confucius was born.

Firecracker label. A boy riding on a Ki Lin was a motif that was occasionally used in artworks and New Year posters. The image represents the birth of righteous sons. Yuen Kee Chun Co., Hong Kong and China, c.1920s.

Firecracker label. Griffin Chop. When used as a trademark for goods exported to the West, the Ki Lin was sometimes referred to as a "griffin," due to the fact that an appropriate English translation was unavailable, or in order to make the creature easier to recognize by relating it to a creature of Western mythology. Early labels often referred to a "chop," in place of the word "brand." This probably originated from the use of the carved chop, or seal that used to be employed as a signature or authentication on documents. Kee Chong Hong, Hong Kong, c.1930.

Tobacco wrapper. Po Lan Tobacco Company, Hong Kong, 1930s.

Firecracker label. *Lee Kwong Yuen Crackers Co.,* Macau, 1930s.

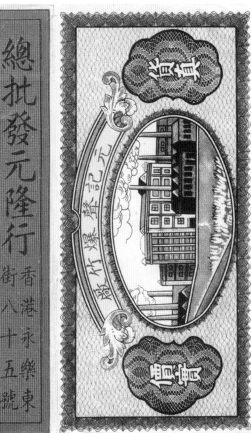

Firecracker wrapper. A Ki Lin issuing forth the Book of Law. The panel at right was designed to enhance the value of the product in the eyes of the consumer. The layout and decorative motifs were taken from paper money designs, while the large, modern factory is an imaginary representation of a firecracker factory. In reality, a traditional firecracker factory would have been a compound containing one story, brick and cement buildings with clay tile roofs, in which workers would perform a series of low-tech, manual tasks until the product was completed. Yuen Loong Hong Firecracker Co., Hong Kong, c.1930s-40s.

Firecracker labels. Various firms used this double-tailed, winged creature as a brand trademark. When mentioned on a label it is generally referred to as a flying bear. The image seems to have been adapted from the mythological creature called "Pixiu." The Pixiu has had varied written descriptions. One portrayed it as having a head like a dragon, a body of a lion, and one horn. Another described it as having the head of a lion, the body of a pig, and one or two antlers. Generally, all have wings or flames issuing from the sides of their bodies. Pixiu were thought to be able to smell money and happily bring it to their master, making it an ideal trademark for an ambitious merchant. Kwong Man Lung Firecracker Co., Hong Kong, c.1920.

A firecracker label from another company of the same period also depicting the floating world, but without the Pixiu. Yuen Kee Kau Co., China, c.1920.

Firecracker label. In this case, the creature translates as a "flying bear." Kung An Tai Co., Buddha Mountain City, Kwangtung, China, 1930s.

Matchbox label. "Flying bear" with one tail. Safety Light Match Co., Ltd., China, c.1920.

Firecracker box panel label. Kwong Hang Shing Co., Kwangtung, China, 1920s.

Firecracker box. Kwong Hang Shing
Co., Kwangtung, China, 1920s.

Firecracker label. Globe Bear Brand. Kwong Hing Tai, Macau, 1950s.

Gods, Deities, and Legendary Figures

Letterhead. Kwan Hing Kee Bean Curd Co., Hong Kong, c.1930s.

Kwan Yin, Goddess of Mercy

Among the most popular of Chinese deities, Kwan Yin is usually depicted as a kind and beautiful woman wearing a white, flowing robe, barefooted, and with a rosary. She is often accompanied by or holding a child, and often has a female attendant by her side. A vase of holy dew is usually by her side or in her hand.

Advertising poster. China Emporium. A beautifully rendered and skillfully printed portrait of Kwan Yin, manufactured in China, for a shop in San Francisco's Chinatown, c.1930s.

Joss sticks labels. Wing Tung Fook. Designed c.1930s; this printing c.1960.

Label. Hong Kong Firecracker Punk Manufacturers. "Punk" is an American term for an incense stick made with few fragrant materials, not made for worship, but for practical uses such as lighting firecrackers or warding off mosquitoes. Hong Kong, 1950s-60s.

Joss sticks label. Tung Fu Hsiang. "One thousand pieces of yellow sandalwood incense." Macau, c.1930s-1950s.

Tea tin. China Beauty. The reverse side has an identical image, but with all Chinese text. South China Tea Corporation Ltd., Hong Kong and China, c.1940s.

Joss stick labels. Leung Wing Shing. (left) Kwan Yin; (right) Kwan Yin or Moon Goddess with white rabbits. Rabbits have a long association with Buddhism and moon mythology. Hong Kong, c.1950s.

Buddha

Po Tai, or Mi Lo Fa has been the most popular form of Buddha for use as a trademark. Known by Westerners as the "Laughing Buddha," he is worshipped for wealth, happiness, and fertility.

Firecracker label. Po Tai is known for his love and generosity toward children. While a mortal, he was known to carry a hemp sack filled with candy for children. The five sons motif shown here implies blessings of fertility. Kwong Man Lung Firecracker Factory, Hong Kong, c.1930.

Firecracker label. Buddha Brand. Hong Kong, 1928.

YEE TIN TONG MEDICAL MANUFACTORY
(PROPRIETORS : YEE TIN TONG. LTD.)
182, QUEEN'S ROAD CENTRAL, HONG KONG

BUDDHA   TRADE MARK

RINGWORM OINTMENT
[FOR EXTERNAL USE ONLY]

Medicine packet, ointment tract, and box. Buddha trademark. Associating the Buddha with a medicinal product was intended to instill extra confidence in the product's effectiveness. *Yee Tin Tong Medical Manufactory, Hong Kong, c.1940s.*

Joss sticks label. *Lee Cheong Hing, Kwangtung and Macau, c.1930s-40s.*

Po Tai has at times been likened to a Santa Claus type figure. A benevolent, jolly old man with a fat belly, a sack of goodies for children, and a fondness for red describes them both. Offerings of food, water, and flowers are made for Po Tai. Cookies and milk are left for Santa. Although no serious suggestion of a historical connection between the two has been proposed, the following labels are interesting examples of cultural intermingling.

Firecracker label. Santa Claus Brand. Santa Claus Brand firecrackers were produced in Kwangtung, China in the 1940s, for export to the U.S. The American importer may have requested the brand name, possibly in response to the tradition of lighting fireworks at Christmas time, particularly in the South. Him Shun Firecracker Co., Kwangtung, China, 1940s.

Joss stick labels. Leung Lan Hing. An identical Santa Claus trademark used on joss stick labels, framed in an ornate border suggesting influence from several periods of Western design. Santa Claus shares this label with Shou Hsing, the star god of longevity. Hong Kong. Designed c.1940s, still in use in 1998.

Joss stick label. Kwang Luen Heng.
Amithaba Buddha. Macau, c.1950s-60s.

Joss sticks label. Chen Kuang Hsing. A meeting of gods, deities, mythological and earthly animals, and monks. The label's text reads: "May the fragrance of the incense penetrate everywhere, to worship all the Buddha's, scholars, saints, and ordinary people, for the salvation of everyone; to promote compassion and to enter the place of enlightenment. One hundred happinesses yellow sandalwood incense." Kwangtung Province, China, early 1900s.

Coil incense label. Hexagonal label used on box lids of small incense coils. The border contains symbolic items associated with the Eight Taoist Immortals. Macau, c.1910s-20s.

Product label. Hsuan Tsang. This label depicts Hsuan Tsang, a famed Tang Dynasty Buddhist master who took a hazardous journey to India to seek the Buddhist scriptures. China or Hong Kong, c.1930s-50s.

Coil incense label. Chan Luen Hing. The figure is a Buddhist monk, possibly Ti Tsang Pusa, who became a legendary figure within the Buddhist pantheon. Chan Luen Hing Joss Sticks Factory, Macau, c.1950s-60s.

Joss sticks label. Ting Choi Kwe. A monk in meditation. Macau, c.1950s.

Joss sticks label. Chan Luen Hing Co., Macau, c.1960s-70s.

Joss sticks label. Kwong Ping On, Hong Kong or Macau, c. 1950s.

Joss sticks label. Leung Wing Shing, Hong Kong and Kwangtung, c.1940s.

Firecracker box label. Moon Goddess. An exquisitely rendered Moon Goddess (Chang O) holds a white rabbit, an animal with strong Buddhist associations. The rabbit on the moon is sometimes depicted grinding ingredients for the Elixir of Longevity, in a mortar. Kwong Lung Co., Fat Shan, Kwangtung, c.1910.

Firecracker label. Moon Brand. Victory Best Firecrackers and Fireworks, Hong Kong, c.1940s.

Box lid. Moon fairy and cash coins trademark. Sam Fong Face Powder Factory. Hong Kong, c.1930s.

Coil incense box lid. Usually built in connection with a temple or monastery, the pagoda is a powerful Buddhist image. Its purpose usually was as a receptacle for religious relics. Wing Tung Fook Co., Hong Kong. Design c.1950s; still in use in the 1990s.

Firecracker label. Heaven and Agricultural Temple Brand. Wong Kwong Hing Co., Tung Cheong Firecracker Factory, Macau, c.1950.

Shou Hsing – The God Of Longevity

The god of longevity, Shou Hsing (also known as Shan Hsing or Lao Shou) has been among the most popular star gods to grace Chinese advertising and label art. Generally depicted as a benevolent old man with a large forehead and white beard, he holds a staff with a bottle gourd tied to it, and/or a giant peach. Often he is in the company of a deer, red bats (usually five), and children.

Shou Hsing is one of three star gods in the heavenly triumvirate known as the Three Pure Ones, which also includes Lu Hsing, the god of wealth and affluence, and Fu Hsing, the god of happiness. The three were often depicted together on New Year posters and other images symbolizing joy and happiness, and were popular subjects in advertising art.

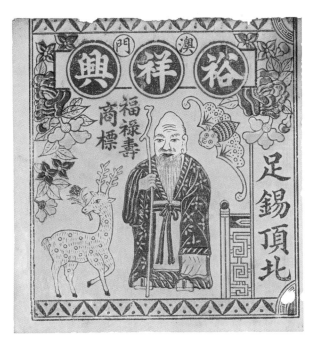

Product label. Lu Hsiang Hsing. Shou Hsing with deer and bat. Macau, c.1920s.

Firecracker label. Five Red Clouds. Shou Hsing is rendered in a traditional style reminiscent of the old New Year posters, in an idyllic setting, surrounded by symbols associated with long life. The characters in the center translate as "five red clouds." Colorful clouds were symbols of peace and good fortune, and were often used as decorative ornaments. Wing Fook Lai, China, 1922.

Firecracker label. Chinook Brand. Themes of longevity—the five bats represent the "Five Blessings" of long life, health, riches, love of virtue, and natural death. Wai Yip Tong, Canton, China 1930s.

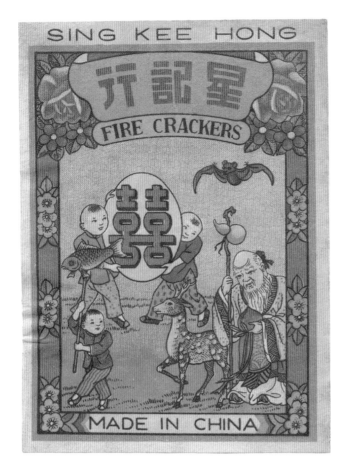

Firecracker label. Sing Kee Hong. The boys carry a huge egg (representing fertility) with a "double happy" character on it. "Double Happy" is a symbolic character used as decoration at weddings, as it is usually associated with a happy marriage. It is also a common good luck symbol. The fish is also a symbol of long life, and as on the label, was carried in processions. China, c.1920s-30s.

Product label or poster. Depiction of the trio of star gods, rendered in a style reminiscent of New Year posters. China, c.1930s-40s.

Firecracker label. Joss Brand. The trio of star gods. Tai Loong, Canton, China 1920s.

Baked goods label. Te Yun Bakery. Amidst festive lanterns and decorations, an
unusual heart-shaped frame surrounds the Three Pure Ones. The scroll reads
"famous courtesy cakes, flaky cakes, and moon cakes." Hong Kong, c.1950s-60s.

Other Gods and Deities

Knitting wool labels. 5 Shoe Sycee Brand. "Shoe sycee" referred to silver or gold ingots cast as currency in China until the 1930s. Also called "boat sycee," they were frequently used in designs and decorations to convey thoughts of wealth. Here, a young boy accompanied by Lu Hsing, the god of wealth (holding a money tree), jumps from sycee to sycee. The reference to the stag comes from the traditional association between Lu Hsing and the stag. South China, late 1920s.

Firecracker label. Lu Hsing, the god of wealth, holds his ru-yi, a form of magic wand that entitles the bearer to fulfilled wishes. Boys frolic among his treasure, pulling gold ingots in front of a vessel containing gold, pearls, cash coins, and other treasures. Po Sing Firecracker Factory, Macau, c.1950.

Fabric label. Incoming Treasure. Traditional rendition of two boys transporting ingots so bright that they emit a flame-like glow. Tu Chang City, China, c.1920.

Advertising poster. China Emporium. Replete with deities, mythological animals, and legendary figures, this poster was used to advertise branches of the China Products Company in Shanghai, Hong Kong, and San Francisco. Shanghai, China, c.1930.

Firecracker label. Diabolo Brand. Lui Kung, the thunder god, is a particularly appropriately choice for a firecracker trademark. One of the few winged Chinese deities, he has the head and claws of a cock, and is always depicted with a hammer and chisel. Here he is running along on large, thunder-producing drums. The "Diabolo" brand name was probably a convenient translation for Westerners who may have associated the appearance of Lui Kung with that of Satan. Yee Cheong Shing Co., Macau, 1920s.

Canned food label. Arrowroot. The trademark is Liu Hai, a benevolent deity associated with prosperity, usually depicted as a young man standing on a 3-legged toad, while swinging a string of coins. Three Star Company, China, c.1940s.

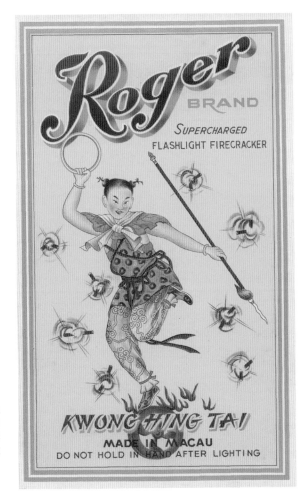

Firecracker label. Roger Brand. The deity used as a trademark for Roger Brand firecrackers was No Cha, a child god able to perform miraculous and heroic deeds with help from his magic bracelet and spear. No Cha moves about by riding his flaming wheel.
Kwong Hing Tai, Macau, c.1950.

Firecracker label. Devil Brand. Like the earlier Diabolo label, this brand was named to give Westerners a frame of reference for an unfamiliar demon-like character. The deity is actually the benevolent Chung Kuei, a form of the god of literature who eventually committed suicide by drowning himself. In one hand, he holds a brush for writing; in the other, a cap worn by high ranking graduating students. Kwong Man Loong, Macau, c.1950.

Firecracker label. Herd Boy and Weaver Girl. An image from the herd boy and the weaver girl story, relating to the Aquila and Vega constellations. According to popular Chinese legend, by a series of circumstances, a weaver girl and herd boy were separated by the girl's father, the sun god, after their marriage. Eventually, they were allowed to meet once a year on the seventh day of the seventh month, and only if it did not rain. The reunion date became a festival day in China. Clear weather was hoped for, as only then would Aquila and Vega (the star constellations that represented the girl and boy) be visible as they crossed paths. The festival was of particular interest to girls, who would watch the sky in order to witness the stars meeting. Witnessing the romantic rendezvous would increase their chances of marrying soon. The label text touts the company's finely made quick-fuse firecrackers, made in a variety of styles. Chi Sheng Hsiang Co., Chiang-Men City, Kwangtung, China, c. early 1900s.

Firecracker label. A later depiction of the herd boy and weaver girl legend. A phoenix carrying exploding firecrackers is added, as is the path of ravens that formed a bridge so that the two could meet. An imaginative Art Deco border surrounds the image. Kwong Hing Cheong Co., China, c.1930.

Firecracker label. Traditional scene depicting the Eight Immortals, a group of Taoist Divinities who achieved immortality by, among other means, drinking the elixir of life. Detailed descriptions of their histories, characteristics, and exploits date to the 1200s. Their popularity within the Chinese pantheon and their compelling imagery has made them a common subject in everything from classic and decorative arts to commercial graphics. Kwong Yuen Co., Macau, early 1900s.

Firecracker label. The fairy Ma Gu, holding a hoe for digging roots of medicinal herbs, and a bamboo pole with a flower basket on the end. A traditional image with Western-influenced border designs. Kwong Man Loong Firecracker Factory, Hong Kong, c.1920.

Tea box. Wo Hop Yee Sin. Traditional scene depicting He He (also known as Ho Ho), heavenly twin boys who symbolize togetherness and harmony. One often holds a lotus or a grain stalk, while the other holds a bowl from which a cloud of steam and good luck bats emerge. The twins are thought of as gods of marriage, and their presence is associated with good omens. Hong Kong, c.1920s.

Cigarette pack. He He. China, c.1930s.

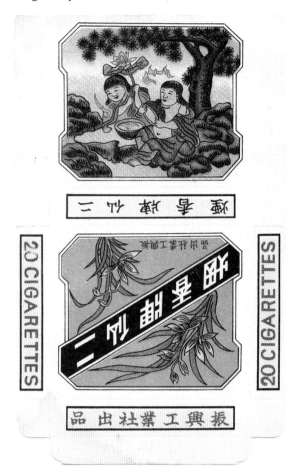

Tea box panel. This trademark is most likely a rendition of He He, yet the figure at right holds a cash coin and is stepping on a three-legged toad. Both characteristics are usually associated with the deity Liu Hai. Yue Mou Co., Hong Kong, c.1930s.

Round tea box lid. Yue Mou Co., Hong Kong, c.1930s.

Wine label. As on many old Chinese labels, two boys hold the banner bearing the company name. On this, the two happen to be He He. The warrior on the flying horse may be a depiction of general Kwan Kong, from the Three Kingdoms story. His horse was described as being able to cover a very long distance in a single leap. China, c.1930s.

EXTRA FINE QUALITY

REGISTERED TRADE MARK
MADE IN HONGKONG

Unusual trademark picturing the Hindu deity Durga, in her Tara form, in a hellish scene of slaughter. Product unknown. Hong Kong, c.1930s-50s.

The Tung Shu is the traditional block-printed Chinese almanac used in determining auspicious days for the correct scheduling of events, and as an all around household reference source. A copy used to be found in most homes, and was replaced with an updated one yearly. Ancient legends told for educational and moral purposes could be found in the Tung Shu, as could information on gods, deities, and their respective natures. The book was a reference guide to Taoist charms, fortune telling and astrology, health issues, face and palm reading, and could be thought of as a compendium of the wisdom of the ancestors. Most of these features were accompanied by fascinating wood block printed illustrations.

Survivals of older editions of the Tung Shu are scarce, as many believed it best to burn or discard the book at the end of the year and replace it with the latest edition. Although it is the oldest continuously published book in the world, it has been altered and added to by artists and experts through the generations. Aside from the obvious updates on astrological information for the coming year, copies printed in twentieth century Hong Kong began to add practical information for use with new technology. For instance, in the latter half of the century the book contained a reference table used in sending transcribed cable messages, showing Chinese characters with numbers assigned to them. With the growing practicality of learning the English language, an illustrated dictionary of commonly used words was included.

Among the most impressive features of the twentieth century Tung Shu was its cover. Publishers adorned it with elaborately illustrated pictures in order to attract buyers and represent the importance of the content. Colorful, beautifully rendered scenes of gods and deities, children at play, pretty women in flamboyant clothing, symbolic and mythological animals, and legendary figures of old were depicted in elaborate settings and lush gardens. The cover pictures were encased in a border often decorated with symbolic motifs and features that frequently combined modern, Western design influences such as Art Deco, with older Chinese motifs.

Other alterations over time were political in nature, and came about as the result of regime or policy change, such as the establishment of China's Communist government in 1949. In a mainland published 1951 edition, the book was given a total makeover, updated, and changed into a politically correct guide to practical and political knowledge from the correct revolutionary perspective. The cover design was completely transformed into a state-sanctioned, modernized scene of utopia in the brand-new era of Communist rule. Rather than attracting buyers with idealized scenes of mythological worlds of the past, the cover of new edition depicted the vision of a bright new China, populated with hard workers who were surrounded by the fruits of their labor. This type of design transformation was to evolve in countless other areas of post-revolutionary Chinese graphic art as well, including advertising and package design. After 1949, printing shops in Hong Kong continued producing the traditional versions of wood block printed almanacs and they are still published annually.

Traditional Chinese almanacs printed in
Hong Kong, c.1940s-1960s.

Almanac cover. People's Republic of China, 1951.

Chapter 3
Westernization and Modernity

For hundreds of years, inspiration for designs on Chinese product labels came from traditional sources such as deities, gods, historical and mythological legends, symbolic animals and supernatural creatures, and age-old border motifs, patterns, and decorations.

During the late nineteenth century, a flow of new perceptions of society and culture was diffusing through Chinese urban centers. Although Western business families and missionaries had long resided in cities such as Canton, Shanghai, Tsingtao, the British colony of Hong Kong, and the Portuguese colony of Macau, it was during the final years of dynastic rule in China that Western cultural, technological, and intellectual influence began to gain significant momentum. The reasons for this are complex, but there were several common motivations. The fascination with new and different things naturally brought on curiosity about foreigners. Most of the foreigners in China were there for business-related reasons, and seemed fabulously wealthy to the average Chinese. Westerners had insights into technology and manufacturing methods that seemed like magical ways to make money.

But China's desire to modernize was motivated by much more than being impressed by Europeans and Americans. Immense economic problems were significantly due to the burgeoning market of Western goods and the financial power of Westerners in China. The history of trade between Western powers and China was fraught with resolutions brought about by the military might of the West. The Opium War, which came about due to China's desire to end forced importation of the narcotic by the British, ended in 1842 with the ceding of Hong Kong to England, and the opium trade left intact. By 1898, regions within China had been ceded to Britain, France, Germany, and Russia. Among the results of this pattern was China's growing concern for strengthening the nation both financially and militarily. Competition for power coincided with competition in business, and the key to success was modernization. It became necessary for the Chinese to even the playing field, and that meant developing industrial and technological abilities that could compete with the modern, developed Western powers.

Ironically, China's acceptance of modernity was actually encouraged by American and European businesses that saw in it a means of increasing their own sales of goods to the Chinese. In the May 1920 issue of *Asia Magazine*, American businessman H.K. Richardson emphasized the need to guide Chinese thinking, in order to sell more American goods:

> "Advertising promotion in China means, first of all, education—to convince that the new is better than the old."

Among the social developments that occurred during the early 1900s was the birth of reform movements. Within the realm of education, the old methods of learning by rote and memorization were giving way to a greater acceptance of imagination and individual expression. This was certainly the case in the world of art education, which had traditionally focused on a learning process requiring attempts by students to duplicate the works of their teacher and the old masters. Often, students would spend several years repeating a single work. Acceptance of individuality and experimentation grew, as interest in Western art techniques expanded. Simultaneously, technical artists became zealous in incorporating Western realism and scientific elements into illustration work.

In major coastal cities such as Shanghai and Canton, design material was obtained through imported books, newspapers, periodicals, and advertisements. By 1912, just after the fall of the Ching Dynasty and the establishment of Republican government, the Shanghai Institute of Fine Art was established. In response to evolving cultural trends, the institute offered a curriculum in both Chinese and Western Art, and became a landmark in the new artistic direction China was taking.

Some Westerners were interested in Chinese aesthetics, especially when it was useful for business purposes. An observation on the importance of packaging design was printed in the May 1931 issue of *China Journal*, a Shanghai publication for expatriate Westerners. It is interesting in that it reflects a desire within Western businesses to cater to what they perceived as Chinese taste:

"It may be argued that such commodities as soap, cosmetics, medicines, children's foods, milk, and the like do not lend themselves to artistic treatment. This is true enough, but they all have to be done up in some kind of packing, and this is precisely where full play may and should be given to the idea of appealing to the Chinese artistic sense. In fact, it is not going too far to say that in merchandising such commodities too much attention to the attractiveness of the packing cannot be given…

"…Wise indeed will be the manufacturer, local or foreign, of almost any article or commodity we may mention, who realizes that his Chinese purchaser has a soul for beauty and will always be more attracted by a thing of artistic value, be it only a wrapper for a cake of soap, than by one that has no appeal in this direction, no matter how useful it may be."

Interaction between China and the West produced a fascinating mixture of styles and influences. On Chinese labels designed during the first half of the twentieth century, we see western subjects and styles from the Victorian era, the Art Nouveau movement, the Art Deco period, and beyond, blended with a host of Chinese religious, symbolic, and decorative elements, all processed through the changing perceptions and realities of time.

Firecracker box label. Despite its traditional subject matter and rendition, this label shows the influence of the European Art Nouveau style in its vine-like border treatment. Kwong Lung Co., Fat Shan, Canton, China, c.1910s.

Tea box panel. Art Nouveau inspired border decorations and Victorian influenced rose decorations adorn this tea label. Ching Mow and Co., Hong Kong, c.1920.

Box panel. Phoenix Brand. "Quick White" polish for whitening shoes and hats. Tai Chung Wah Co. Hong Kong, Macao, and Canton China, c.1930.

Printing and dying factory label. Family Brand. "Products so good they are sold in both hemispheres"; "Flowery colors that stay bright as the sun." Tsingtao, China, 1930s.

Book cover. Entwined Dragon Treasure Fan. Ng Kwai Tong (Five Cassia Hall), Publisher. Hong Kong, c. 1950s.

美唱牌

美昌工廠 上海

Mei Chon

Mei Chong Knitting Works Shanghai China

Knitwear box. Fashion, sex, and technology used in advertising. Mei Chon Knitting Works, Shanghai, China, c.1930.

Phonograph record and sleeve. Printed on back of sleeve: "Reproduce the best music by the most famous artists in China. They are excellent for listening to and as a complement for dancing. Foreigners will not fail to appreciate them." New Moon Gramophone and Record Co., Shanghai, Hong Kong, and Canton, China, c.1920s-30s.

Phonograph record and sleeve. Recorded and designed in China, manufactured in USA for distribution in China and other areas of large Chinese population. Oriental Record Co., c.1920s-30s.

Lyrics pamphlets
included with
Chinese opera
records. Brunswick
Record Co. (USA) of
Hong Kong, 1930s.

Catalog graphics. Brunswick Record Co., Hong Kong, 1930s.

Cigarette advertisement. Wing Tai Vo
Tobacco Corp., China, 1920s-30s.

Watermelon seed packet. Unlicensed adaptation of the Superman™ comic-book character from America. Manila, Philippines, c.1940s-50s.

Firecracker labels. Two versions of "Wristwatch Brand" firecrackers. Wing Lee Lung Firecracker Co., China, c.1940s.

Ginger tin side panel. Evening factory silhouettes. Amoy Ginger Co., Hong Kong, c.1940s-50s.

Shopping bag. Fung Yue
Oyster Sauce Co., Hong
Kong, c.1950s.

Masthead and advertisement from harmonica
enthusiast's magazine. Shanghai, China, 1949.

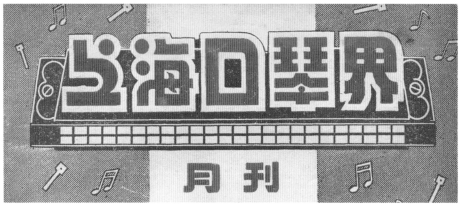

Magazine advertisement.
Shanghai, China, 1951.

Advertising poster. Three-horse-head brand cotton shirts—"excellent quality, reasonable prices." Kwanghua textile factory, China, c.1940s-50s.

Shopping bag. Labour Brand. Yee Yee and Co. Chinese Wine and Spirits, Macau, c.1950s.

Shopping bag. Medicinal Wine. "Fragrant, gives energy, enriches blood, maintains complexion." Lien Sheng Winery, Hong Kong, c.1950s.

Medicine packet. Three Hand Brand Headache
Powder. King Wah Drug Co. Singapore, 1950s.

Lichee box end panel. Thumb Brand. Hong Kong, 1960s.

Memo book. Hong Kong, 1961.

Chinese Opera record. Lucky Record
Co., Hong Kong, 1950s.

永安唐樓

永安建築有限公司
九龍豉油街九十四號
電話：
五九五九一
五九九六四

康樂街

快富街

上海街

Real estate promotion folder. Hong Kong, c.1960.

CHOW HSUAN

麗鳴
快唱

Liming RECORD

Record. Pop songs by singer
Chow Hsuan. Liming Records,
Hong Kong, c. late 1950s.

Chapter 4
Art Deco

During the 1920s and '30s, the blossoming European and American Art Deco movement had an enormous influence on Chinese art and advertising. Used for decades after its peak in Europe and America, the style's whimsical use of geometric ornamentation became a fixture in the modern Chinese advertising aesthetic. The influence of Art Deco in China was largely facilitated by imported European and American published material.

Some of the most striking of the label designs from this period were those combining traditional Chinese elements with Art Deco influenced borders and decorative work. Chinese subject matter surrounded by abstract, geometric designs that radiated modernity and technology was an ironic, yet very successful blend.

Firecracker label. Angel Brand. Kwong Man Lung Firecracker Factory. Hong Kong, 1930s-40s.

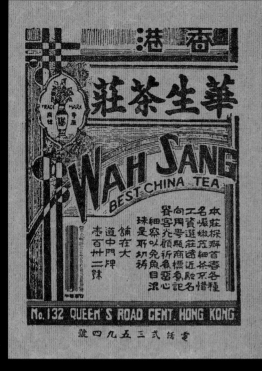

Letterhead. Nam Yang Fire-Crackers Co., Macau, c.1940s.

Tea label. Wah Sang Best China Tea.
Hong Kong, c.1930s-40s.

Ink bottle and box. Kwong Yuen Co., Hong Kong, 1930s.

Cigarette paper. Gorilla Brand. The Great Wall
Industry, Singapore, c.1930s.

Tea box panels. Ying Mee Tea Co., Hong Kong, c.1930s.

Firecracker label. Double Girls.
Kwong Hang Shing Co.,
Kwangtung, China, c. 1930s.

Incense label. A medley of geometric forms and stylized plants. Lee Cheong Hing Co., Macau. Designed c.1930s; still in use in the 1990s.

Tea tin. Kean Thye Tea Merchant. Penang, Malaysia, 1940s.

Song book cover. "Reborn Flower / Newest Famous Cinema Songs." Shanghai, c.1930s.

精製名香　選料上乘

芳芬馥郁　與眾不同

陳聯馨富貴長壽香

本莊創設九十餘年承辦　箱香專銷南洋美洲各埠

貨式精美取價公平各種　名香零沽批發一律歡迎

總批發
香港大道西
式百四十一號
電話：五〇
四九六八七五

Incense labels. Chan Luen Hing Co., Hong Kong. Designed c.1930s-1950s; still in use in the 1990s.

陳聯馨萬壽香

CHAN LUEN HING BEST QUALITY JOSS STICK

總批發
香港大道西四一式號
電話：四九六八七五

大新公司

專各國名廠呢絨定頭中眼服沽零批辦

澳門草堆街第五號

澳門新步頭泰興印刷所承印

Clothing box. Macau, 1930s.

72

Firecracker label. Ki Lin. Chee Hing Lung Co., China, c.1930s-50s.

Dried lichees box lid and end panel. Kwong Sang Loong, Canton, China, 1930s.

Panel labels of the 1930s.
Canton and Macau.

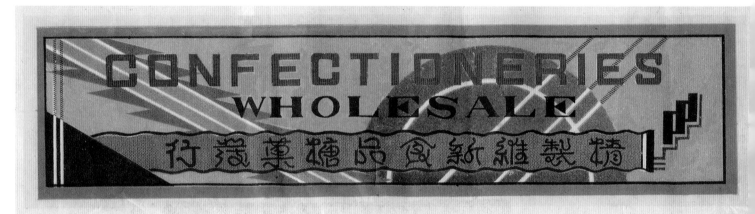

行發菓糖品食新維製增

昇爆寶
竹
爆紅一第
包十四排雙
等超

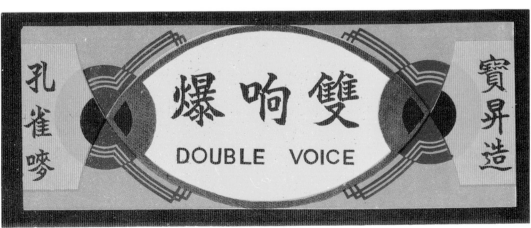

孔雀嘜 爆响雙 寶昇造

DOUBLE VOICE

Shopping bag. Soi Cheong Provisions. Macau, c.1950s.

Harmonica magazine advertisement. Shanghai, 1949.

Firecracker label. Man Chong Co., Macau, 1950s.

Tea tin. Flying Horse Brand. Unlicensed use of the Mobil Oil™ trademark. Fukien Tea Co., Hong Kong, 1950s.

Sauce label. Wing Tai Sharp Sauce. Hong Kong, c.1950s(?). In use during the 1990s.

The Kwan Yick, Yick Loong, and Wang Yick Fireworks Companies used some of the finest examples of Chinese Art Deco labels. The three businesses were closely associated, and may actually have been branches of one company.

Hex-pack firecracker label. Cock Brand. Kwun Yick (Kwan Yick) Fireworks Co., Canton and Macau, 1930s.

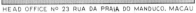

Firecracker labels. Kwan Yick and Yick Loong Fireworks Companies. Most likely designed by the same artist. 1940s-50s.

Three labels from Duck Brand "celebration string" boxes of firecrackers. Yick Loong Fireworks Co., Macau, c.1930s.

Firecracker labels. Wang Yick (Camel
Brand), Kwan Yick (Cock Brand), and
Yick Loong (Duck Brand). Macau, 1950s.

Chapter 5
Women in Chinese Advertising

Portraits of beautiful women were a staple of Chinese advertising art during the first half of the twentieth century. The "golden age" was in the 1920s and '30s, the period when "Meinu Yufenpai," or "Beautiful Woman Calendar Poster," reigned as China's most highly developed form of printed advertising to date. The central component of these posters was the image of one or more beautiful women in a myriad of idyllic, often dreamlike settings.

From the teens through the 1930s, commercial calendar art was China's paramount printed advertising form. The genre's artistic hub was Shanghai, China's preeminent metropolis at the time, and its foremost center of Chinese/Western cultural intermingling.

Chinese and foreign companies that produced goods such as textiles, cigarettes, cosmetics, medicines, beer, batteries, etc., kept the studios busy designing Meinu Yufenpei. The Beautiful Woman Calendar Poster genre evolved into a sophisticated form of commercial art, rendered by accomplished, professional artists. Their designs took many elements from traditional Chinese sources, notably, nianhua (New Year pictures), but also employed interpretations of Victorian, Art Nouveau, and Art Deco styles as well as Western painting and illustration techniques. In many cases, women were depicted in traditional clothing and in olden surroundings, but what most characterized this genre were the idealized images of modern urban Chinese women.

Shanghai was the center of China's early women's movement, and the work from local design studios reflects the transformation of women's roles. The women depicted on the Meinu Yufenpai were independent and expressive, confident, gorgeous, and engaged in all sorts of pastimes previously found only in Europe and America.

Not surprisingly, the novel and impressive artwork on these posters influenced other commercial art forms, such as label and trademark graphics. Charming young women in traditional or modern Western clothing could be seen on packages of all kinds of products from cities such as Shanghai, Canton, Hong Kong, and Macau, and for decades after the age of Meinu Yufenpai.

Product label. Ma Family Company, probably textile manufacturers. Shantung Province, China, c.1920s.

Fabric label. Two Girls. China, c.1920.

Firecracker label. Earth Brand. Wong Kwong Hing Co.,
Kwangtung Province, China, c.1920.

Dried lichees box. Hing Chan Produce
Factory, Hong Kong, 1960s.

Tea tin label. Chan Chun Lan Tea
Merchants, Hong Kong, c.1950s.

Joss sticks label. Traditionally dressed maiden. China, c.1930s-40s.

Joss sticks label. Maiden wearing cheongsam. China, c.1930s-40s.

Product label. China, 1920s.

Joss sticks label. Ladies wearing cheongsam. Canton and Hong Kong, c.1920s.

Firecracker label. The vertical characters read:
"The Beauty of Spring." Hsun Tien Hsiang Co.,
Hsin Chang City, China, 1920s.

Firecracker label. Earth Brand. Wong Kwong Hing
Fireworks, Kwangtung, China, c.1930.

Powder tin. The double girl trademark was used by the
Kwong Sang Hong Co. from its establishment in 1905,
and underwent several transitions through the ensuing
decades. On this face powder tin, the girls are wearing
1910s-1920s style cheongsam. KSH was among the
most successful cosmetic companies in the Far East,
and advertised profusely through the beautiful woman
picture calendars. Hong Kong, c.1930s.

Clothes box lid. Nan Hai, China, c.1920s.

Textiles label.
Beauty Brand.
Hsieh Hsin Factory,
China, late 1920s.

Tea tin label. Fu Tseng Chun Tea Firm,
Shantung Province, China, c.1930s.

Hand Gestures

"In Chinese traditional painting the hands and fingers, like the eyes, were painted with expression. In calendar posters the hands of beautiful women are painted in varying poses: extended, closed, bent, uplifted, etc. They were windows to the subjects' inner worlds as well as expressions of their intentions and dispositions." (Warren Leung, ed., *Chinese Women and Modernity*, 1996).

Firecracker label. Earth Brand. Wong Kwong Hing Co., Kwangtung, China, 1930s.

Clothes box lid. China, 1930s.

Original artist's layout and label. Kwong Hing Tai Firecracker Co., Macau, 1930s.

Firecracker label. Yick Loong Firecracker Factory, Macau, 1930s.

Tea box. Luen Chong Tai Tea Merchant, Hong Kong, 1930s.

Firecracker advertising poster. Kwong Man Loong Firecracker Factory, Hong Kong, mid 1930s.

Tea box. Kwong Sang Co., Hong Kong, 1930s.

Firecracker label. Chan Thye Yick. Made in China for the Malaysian market, 1930s.

Tea tin. Tung Kee & Co., Shanghai, 1930s.

Stock advertising flyer. This small poster or label is an example of a generic design on which a business could put customized text. Hong Kong or China, 1930s.

Advertising flyer. The Spring Peach Garden Tea House, offering homemade fashionable and seasonal cakes and snacks, and specializing in a variety of famous teas. China, 1930s.

Tea box. Wing Shun Tea Co., Hong Kong, 1930s.

Firecracker label. Sam Yick
Firecracker Factory, China, 1930s.

Advertising poster. Canton Importing Co.,
Portland, Oregon. Printed in China, c. 1930.

Tea house label/flyer. Ho Chan Tea House.
"Famous tea known everywhere; excellent snacks;
fried noodles; wedding cakes; all kinds of fried
dishes; Western baked goods." Macau, 1930s.

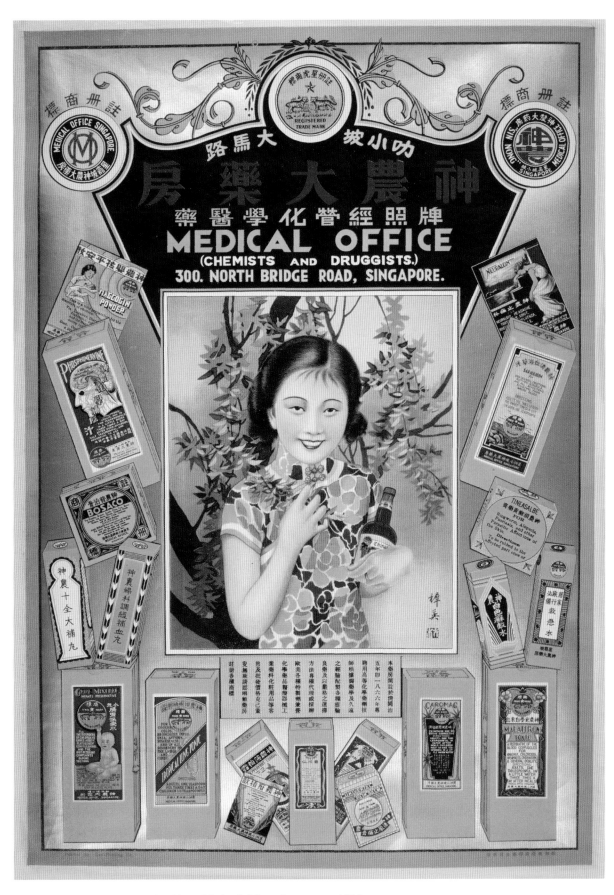

Druggist advertising poster. Sin Nong Medical Office, Singapore, 1930s.

Baked goods labels. Hong Kong, c. 1930s.

Lichee box lids of the era were heavily influenced by the calendar art of the day. Modern, beautiful women were depicted in well-rendered borders and frames on some of the most impressive packages ever produced in China.

Dried lichees boxes. Canton, China, 1930s.

Fabric label. Seaside Beauty. Yung Yi Silk and Cotton Weaving and Dyeing Factory, Tsingtao, China, c.1950s.

Swallow's nest boxes. Swallow's nest soup is a rare and expensive delicacy, and said to have beneficial effects on one's health. Boxes of nests often had a cellophane window so the product could be displayed. Hong Kong, c.1930s-50s.

Box lid. Jab Tai Choon. Traditional Chinese writing brushes and ink. Hong Kong, 1930s-40s.

Tea box. Yue Mou Tea Co., Hong Kong, c.1930s-50s.

Tea tin. Heung Chan Tea Firm, Hong Kong, 1950s.

Tea tin. Tung Yu Yuen Tea
Merchant, Hong Kong, 1950s.

Advertising poster. Ling Chi Medicine Co.
Tradition and progress. Hong Kong, 1950s.

Bakery label/advertisement. Te Yun Chia Cake
House., Hong Kong, 1950s.

Tea box. Mee Chun Tea Co., Hong Kong, 1950s.

stry tin. Fung Wong Rolls. Hong To Yuen Co.,
ong Kong, 1950s-1960s.

贈敬號布成順門祁

抗美援朝
保家衛國
花色齊全
歡迎賜顧

Fabric poster. Hsun Cheng Pu Hao Fabric
Store. In the early to mid 1950s, advertising
posters still reflected much of the Shanghai
poster style. The text informs us that flower-
colored fabric is being sold, and that custom-
ers are most welcome. The poster also carries slogans telling citizens to oppose America,
aid North Korea, and protect the homeland
and its families. Chi-men, China, early 1950s.

abel and advertisement. Te Yun Old Bakery. Hong Kong, c.1960s.

得雲老餅家

Magazine advertisement.
Lemonin Worm Powder.
Hong Kong, 1957.

Chapter 6
Children in Chinese Advertising

Children have always been popular subjects in Chinese art and advertising. Generally depicted as happy, cute, and charming, they represented an optimistic outlook toward the future. But in understanding the role of children in Chinese advertising it is important to bear in mind the deeply rooted traditional belief that a boy was superior to a girl. When a boy was born, it was cause for jubilation and family pride, but when a girl was born, no matter how well loved she was, there was a degree of disappointment, as it was the boy who would continue to propagate the clan, inherit the family's land, and perform rituals to honor ancestors. A girl would marry into her husband's family and become part of it, assuming worship duties for her husband's ancestors rather than her own, her primary purpose being to bear and raise his children. Boys were associated with the most positive connotations, and so in traditional advertising art, they were portrayed almost exclusively.

The reform movements that began in the 1920s played a significant role in China's efforts to transform attitudes regarding gender. Growing acceptance of Western ideas and the subsequent desire to modernize eventually led, at least in urban areas, to improved education opportunities for girls, a less demeaning role in the family, and more promise for future jobs. As attitudes began to change, girls were seen more often on posters and in advertising.

As of 1949, with the Communist system in place, the official intention to elevate the status of peasants brought with it an effort to raise the status of girls and women. As family real estate was no longer an issue under Communism, and religious rituals were now officially discouraged, the importance of the male as heir and religious spokesman diminished. The party's official stance was that people of all classes and genders were equally entitled to opportunities and the benefits of progress. Artists and designers were now instructed to depict girls and women as comrades who shared the responsibilities of everything from manual labor to military duty.

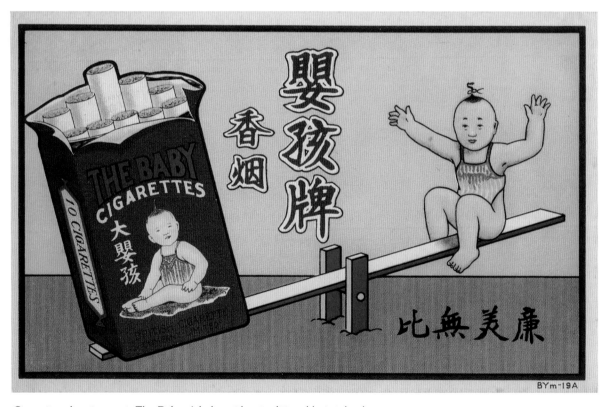

Cigarette advertisement. The Baby. A baby with a traditional hairstyle plays on a seesaw opposite a freshly opened pack of cigarettes. Emblematic of its implied value, the pack outweighs him. British Tobacco Co., Shanghai, China, c.1930.

Receipt banner. Baby sitting on a "double happy" character. The double happy symbol is actually a character much used as a motif, symbolizing happy marriage and long life. Crystallized or preserved fruit factory. Hong Fa Hsing Po Chi Company, Hong Kong, 1930s-50s.

Cigarette pack label. Baby carriage. China, c.1930s-50s.

Bakery advertising poster. "A fashionable variety of cakes, deserts, and snacks." The decorative fruits on the border have symbolic connotations of fertility, wealth, and long life. Pa Mien City, China, c.1930s.

Dry ginger tin. Amoy Canning Corp., Hong Kong, c.1940s-50s.

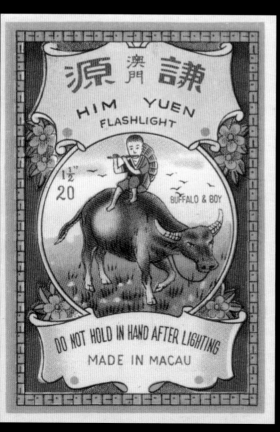

Firecracker label. Buffalo & Boy. Him Yuen Firecracker Factory, Macau, early 1950s.

Advertising poster/label. New China Dying and Weaving Co., China, c.1930s.

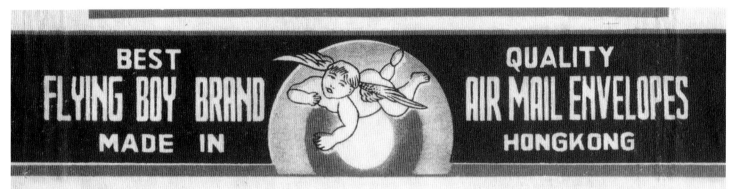

Envelope band. Flying Boy Brand. Hong Kong, 1950s.

Business card. Happy Medicine Co., Macau, c.1950s-60s.

Tea box panel. Woo Long Tea. Yue Mow Tea Co., Hong Kong, c.1930s.

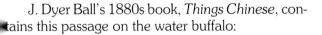

Fabric Label. Flying Baby Brand. China National Textiles Import and Export Corporation, People's Republic of China, 1950s.

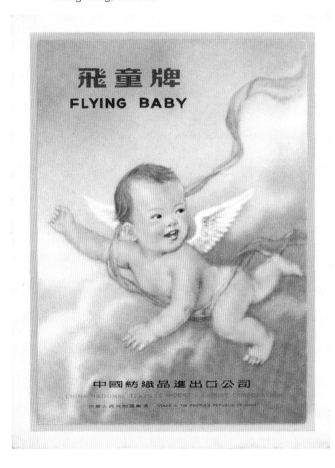

J. Dyer Ball's 1880s book, *Things Chinese*, contains this passage on the water buffalo:

"The buffalo is a dangerous animal for Europeans to approach…but with its friends is thoroughly docile, and in perfect control of the little boys who have the task of driving them to and from the fields, and of guiding them when pulling the harrow and plough, often riding on their backs. So common is this sight that the metaphor of a lad astride a buffalo's back, blowing the flute…appears in painting and is used for decorative designs, etc."

Brand Evolution: Double Happy Brand

Firecracker label. Double Happy Brand. With symbols of happiness and longevity, and under Mom's supervision, boys with modern Western clothing and traditional Ching Dynasty hairstyles celebrate the New Year. Kwong Man Long (sic) Co., Hong Kong, 1920s.

A version from the 1950s, in which traditional clothes are worn.

Another 1950s version: a transformation into modernity. Up to date clothing, girls are included, and the fish, symbolic of long life, has been replaced with a bunch of balloons.

Incense label. Boys riding carps. The heavenly abode is not overlooked in this Art Deco framed scene of boys riding carps, a traditional image of good luck. The flag reads "number one fragrance." Wing Tung Fook Incense Co., Hong Kong. Design c. 1930s, still in use in the 1990s.

Fireworks label. Yick Lung Firework Co. This early Yick Lung label is an odd combination of motifs and styles. Border designs exhibit a mixture of Art Nouveau and Art Deco influences; flowers, checkerboard patterns, and an early photo of Mr. Tang Pick (sic) Tong surround a charming moonlight scene of children having fun with fireworks. Macau, c.1930.

Textile machinery advertising poster. Boy Scouts Brand. The Boy Scouts were established in China in 1913. Here, representing a bright future for China, they advertise machinery and supplies for printing and dying fabric. Shanghai, China, 1930s.

Advertising poster. Football Brand. Hand-knitted articles of clothing made of sheep's wool. China, c.1930s.

Firecracker label. Triple Happy. For emphasis, an extra "happiness" is added to the more common "double happy." The characters at bottom assure "repeating sounds of reporting good news." Nan Hai Firecracker Factory, Nan Hai, China, early 1950s.

Firecracker label. A woman shows a scroll proclaiming the fine quality of the product. Kwong Yuen Hang Kee Firecracker Factory, Macau, 1950s.

Advertising poster. "Innocent Pleasure."
Stock advertisement for a bleach and dye
factory. Tsingtao, China, early 1950s.

Advertising poster for herbal medicine. In a
scene reminiscent of the Ching Dynasty, a
woman teaches her son to write with a reed,
in a pile of spilled grain. He is writing names
of the company's products. World Great Pharmacy Central Headquarters, Shantung Province, China, c.1920s-30s.

Firecracker label. Superior Mandarin. A riotous New Year celebration, filled with symbolic icons of good luck and long life, and many sons. Hunan Fireworks Factory, Hunan, China, c. early 1960s.

Children's book cover. Two exemplary uniformed boys, walking home from school, and still interested in reading. Shanghai, 1920s.

Advertising poster. Fu Hsing Tea Store. A woman in a stylish cheongsam holds a rose while she walks with a young, uniformed student along a lakeside bamboo grove. This was most likely a "stock label," one of many generic designs on which a business could put customized text. Hsin Chen, China, c.1930.

Children's Writing Practice Books

Printed in Hong Kong and distributed to Chinese communities the world over, children's character writing practice books had a variety of printed scenes on their covers, intended to appeal to school children. These date to the 1950s-60s.

Children's writing practice books, printed in Hong Kong, c. 1950s-60s.

This writing practice book was printed in the People's Republic of China during the Cultural Revolution (1966-1976). With the purposeful demeanor of red guards, students hold up copies of *Quotations from Chairman Mao Zedong*.

Chapter 7
The Animal Kingdom

Animals provided subject matter for Chinese advertising and packaging from earliest times. Their visual images and symbolic associations made for an unlimited source of advertising power. Flowers and plants further added to the positive nature of the illustrations, as well as the symbolic and decorative beauty of the design.

In old Chinese belief, animals had so many symbolic associations and mysterious powers that one wonders just how much of a distinction was made between mythological creatures and animals whose existence could be confirmed by mortals who had actually seen them. It is likely that the line was thin, for in earlier times all were thought to be real. Perhaps animals such as the dragon and phoenix were thought of as being elusive, on a higher plane of reality, but no less real than a water buffalo or tortoise.

Gift envelope. This decorative envelope was used to present a gift of money at New Year time. The inscription contains the name of the recipient, and expresses a gracious request for him to accept the gift. Macau, c.1940s-50s.

Medicinal plaster packet. Penang, Malaysia, c.1930s-40s.

Advertising flyer. Eng Aun Tong Headache Cure. Tiger Balm, made by medicine company Eng Aun Tong, is the most widely known of the myriad of ointments and balms manufactured in Asia. Chinese herbalist Aw Chu Kin, of Fujian province, established Eng Au Tong (Hall of Everlasting Peace) in Rangoon, Burma. In 1926, eighteen years after his death, his son Aw Boon Haw relocated the company to Singapore, where it became hugely successful. This leaflet touts the company's headache remedy. Singapore, 1930s.

Reverse of Eng Aun Tong flyer.

Insect repellant incense box lid. Considered the king of all the wild beasts, the tiger was also thought to be capable of scaring away evil spirits. Its image has been represented on an array of items, for the sake of protection. Kwangtung, China, c.1930s-40s.

Headache cure packet. Ngoi Kum Sam. Although not indigenous to China, the lion has long been regarded as a defender of the law and a protector of buildings. The male lion was often depicted playing with an ornamental ball. This gave rise to the popular lion and globe motif, used as a trademark for countless Chinese products throughout the twentieth century. Singapore, c.1930s-40s.

Matchbox label. Lion Globe. Tung Hing Co., Macao and Kwangtung, China, c.1920.

Soy sauce label. Wa Chun Co., Hong Kong, 1930s.

Firecracker label. Early incarnation of Po Sing's long running Lion Globe trademark. Po Sing Firecracker Factory, Canton, China and Hong Kong, c.1920s-30s.

Firecracker label. Mandarin ducks, symbolic of marital felicity and faithfulness, were a popular motif in Chinese advertising and art. Kwong Hang Seng Co., China, c.1940s.

Reworked version of Po Sing's Lion Globe trademark. Macau, 1950s.

Tea box panel label. Ying Mee Tea Co., Hong Kong, c.1940s.

Firecracker label and artist's draft. The deer is among the most symbolically significant of Chinese animals. Believed to live to a great age, it was often shown in the company of Shou Hsing, the god of longevity. The deer is the only animal able to find the ling chih, the fungus of immortality. This artist's label draft was prepared for the Kwong Hing Tai firecracker company of Macau. The actual label shown is a version adapted for use by the Yick Loong firecracker company, also of Macau. c.1930s.

Firecracker label. Wing Hang Firework Co., Macau, early 1950s.

Firecracker label. Koong Chong Kat & Co. The monkey and wasps motif represents a prestigious promotion. This interpretation is based on puns and cultural symbolism: the Chinese word for "wasps" rhymes with "to entitle," while the word for monkey rhymes with the title of a high level official. Wasp nests were a symbol of official authority, as they resembled chops, or carved stamping blocks used to sign documents. This rendition includes a peach in the monkey's hand, a symbolic motif unto itself. Together with the deer and pine tree, a message of long life is also conveyed. Canton, China, c.1920s.

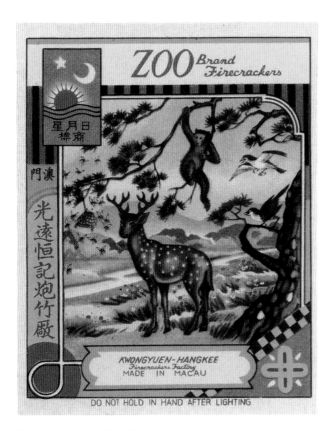

Firecracker label. Zoo Brand. Later version, showing Western influence on the border design as well as within the image itself. Kwongyuen Hangkee Firecracker Factory, Macau, early 1950s.

Medicinal tea packet. Chu Hsiang Chye. A deer eating ling chih made an ideal trademark for a medicinal product. The design on this herb tea packet probably dates to the 1930s, and was in use for several decades. Note the roof shaped border around the lower text. China, c.1940s.

Firecracker label. Man Chong Co. Hong Kong, c.1940s-50s.

Shopping bag. The image of two deer was an appropriate design to represent a ginseng shop, as ginseng has long been associated with health, vitality, and longevity. Macau, c.1950s.

Medicinal balm packet. Deer with ling chih, the fungus of immortality, in its mouth. China, c.1960s.

Matchbox label. Cheong Ming Match Co, Macau, c.1930.

Powder packet. Birds of many types were popular subjects in label and trademark art. Bird species were associated with particular flowers and were often illustrated with them. Song Fon Powder Factory, China, c.1930s.

Matchbox label. Swallows Brand. Manufactured in China for the Malaysian market. c.1950s.

Tea box panels. Ying Mee Tea Co., Hong Kong, c.1930s.

Matchbox label. Shang Yan. People's Republic of China, late 1950s.

Phonograph record. Chinese Record Co. Cockatoos trademark. Shanghai, China, 1910s-20s.

Ointment box. Parrot Brand. Sui Cheong Medicine Co., Ltd. Hong Kong, c.1950s.

Firecracker box. Parrot Brand. Him Son Firecracker Factory, Macau, early 1950s.

Tea tin. Three Eagles trademark. Eagles are symbolic of strength. When shown with a pine tree, as in this design, connotations of longevity are added. The auspicious number three further compounds the symbolic nature of the design. Ying Mee Tea Co., Hong Kong, c.1920.

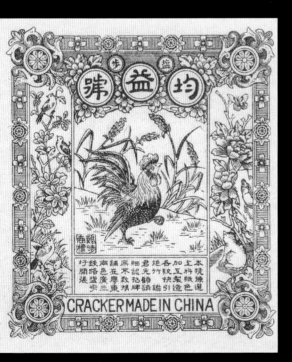

Firecracker label. Cock Brand. In ancient Chinese texts, the cock was believed to possess the "five virtues": literacy, fighting ability, courage, benevolence, and faithfulness. The cock was also symbolic of the sun, due to its habit of crowing at daybreak. Crowing was thought to scare away evil spirits, as ghosts would go to sleep at dawn. This early design frames the cock's image with birds, flowers, butterflies, and a cat, all framed within a Western-style stock border. Kwan Yick Firecracker Co., Kwangtung, China, c.1920.

Firecracker label. Cock Brand. Kwan Yick Fireworks Co. Kwangtung, China, c.1920.

Canned food label. Pork Cooked With Sauce. Swatow Food
Canning Co., Swatow, China, c.1950.

Firecracker label. Goldenfish Brand. Because of its phonetic
similarity to the word for abundance, the fish is often used to
symbolize prosperity. Kwongyuen Hangkee Firecrackers
Factory, China, c.1940s.

Detail from medicine tract. Chin Ken Ip. Bat trademark
rendered in traditional Chinese stylized form. Bats were
regarded as good omens. They symbolize longevity (especially in groups of five), prosperity, happiness, and good luck.
Hong Kong, c.1930.

Dried ginger label. Choy Heong Co.,
Hong Kong, c.1930s-50s.

Detail from medicine tract. Although combinations of two different animals are not uncommon in Chinese trademarks, the bat and clam duo is very unusual. Yeung Lau Sin Medicine Co., Hong Kong, c.1930s-40s.

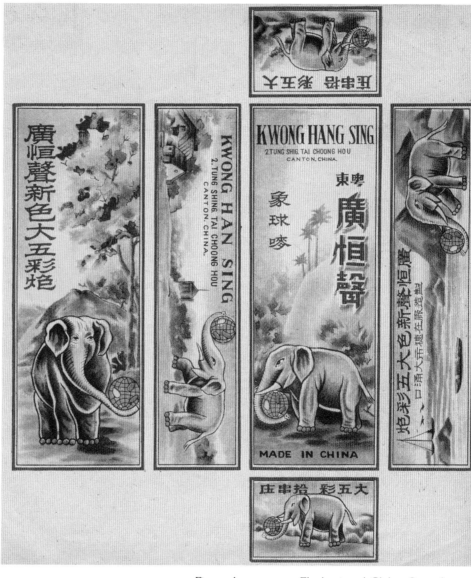

Fireworks label. Fei Tin Brand. This elephant is traditionally garbed and ornamented, and set against a background of modernity and industrialization. Hunan Fireworks Factory, Hunan, China c. early 1960s.

Firecracker wrapper. Elephant and Globe. One of many Chinese trademarks that utilized the globe to emphasize the wide range of the consumer market controlled by a firm. The use of the elephant emphasizes power and strength. Kwong Hang Sing, Canton, China, c.1930s.

Chapter 8
Transportation

The Chinese junk was used as a trademark or label subject for a myriad of products. Generally, it was shown in front of a coastline, or in serene ocean settings, often in front of a sunset, with a few gulls trailing behind. The junk was a common, but beautiful boat, propelled for centuries only by wind and waves. It was emblematic of tradition, craftsmanship, and continuity.

Modern transportation technology, on the other hand, provided advertising inspiration through its connotations of progress, industry, power, and speed. The image of a fast, brand new train, airplane, car, or boat provided an electrifying image, implying that the manufacturer was progressive and successful. From the 1910s on, exciting depictions of machine-powered vehicles were used to sell many Chinese products.

Shopping bag. Chinese junk. Man Lee Joss Stick Co., Macau, c. 1950s.

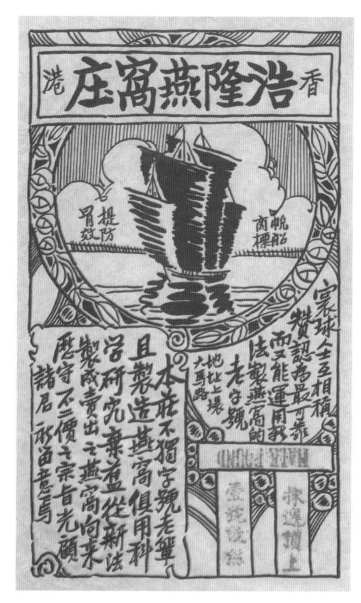

Swallow's nest wrapper. Fan Chuan Co., Hong Kong, c.1930s-50s.

Firecracker label. Chin Teow Heng. Penang, Malaysia, c.1930s-50s.

Firecracker label. "Cha Mo Co" Brand. The inspiration behind this label's design was the "Junk Stamp" of the Chinese postal system. Among the first stamps issued by the Republic of China, it was in use from 1913-1924. Ironically, the Junk Stamp was designed and engraved by Lorenzo Hatch, an American. Canton, China, c.1920s-30s.

Wine label. Soi Foong Co., Macau, c.1950s.

Tea box panel. A Chinese ship leaves a British port (Hong Kong?) amidst sentimental farewells. Kwong Sang Tea Co., Hong Kong, 1930s.

Fabric label. Imaginative early air travel. East Asia Fabric Factory, Macau, c. 1910s-20s.

Firecracker labels. Kwan Yick Fireworks Factory, Macau (left) and Kwangtung (right), 1920s.

Receipt letterhead.
Choy Hop Sang Kee
Co., Hong Kong,
1930s.

Firecracker label. Po Cheong Lung Co., Hunan, China, c.1940s.

Tea tin. *Kee Tin Tea Co., Fukien, China, 1940s.*

Firecracker label. A stylish girl rides her bike through a lush setting. Tai Wah Hau Co., China, 1930s-40s.

Fabric label. Shenyang City Machine Dyeing Factory, Mukden, Liaoning Province (Manchuria), China, c.1940s.

Tea packet. Tick Kwan Yin Co., Hong Kong, 1950s.

Cigarette pack label. A Chinese airplane flies over an industrious, modern city (perhaps Shanghai). People's Republic of China, 1950s.

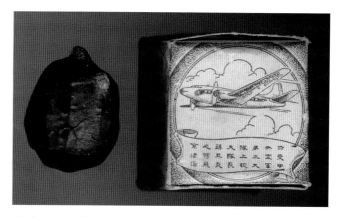

Medicine box for traditional, wax-coated pill. Shanghai, c.1940s.

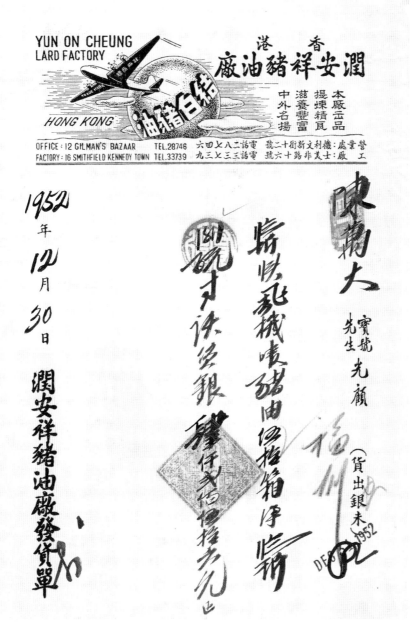

Receipt. The airplane is an interesting contrast to the traditional chop stampings and the old style vertical writing. Yun On Cheung Lard Factory, Hong Kong, 1952.

Fabric sampler cover. Bright Like New Weaving, Printing, and Dying Factory, Ltd., PRC, 1950s.

Stock graphic for printed items. PRC, 1976.

Matchbox label. Motorcar Safety
Matches. China, c.1950.

Firecracker label. Superior Mandarin.
The Yangtze Bridge in Nanjing was built
in the 1960s and became an icon in
Chinese commercial and propaganda art
of the Cultural Revolution. Hunan,
China, c.1970.

Chapter 9
Patriotism and the Military

Political statements are often expressed in commercial art, whether through the presence of a flag, slogan, or trademark, or a message implied through its graphics. Military might has always been a popular theme as well. Many Chinese labels had designs based on the need or desire to show allegiance to a particular political direction. Warriors from dynastic periods have been commemorated on countless labels printed before the mid twentieth century.

After the 1911 victory by Sun Yat Sen, and concurrent demise of the dynastic system, up to date political symbols and soldier portraits greatly increased in use. With the establishment of the Chiang Kaishek's Nationalist Government in 1928, the use further increased, as did modern combat scenes.

The incorporation of flags in label design was a simple way for a merchant or manufacturer to proclaim political loyalty, and to promote consumption of domestic goods. When it came to export goods, juxtaposing or crossing the Chinese flag with the flag of the country importing the goods was a popular way to express friendly relations and, hopefully, increase sales.

Recognition of flags is often helpful in narrowing down the time period during which an item was printed. The earliest examples of the use of a Chinese national flag in advertising seem to have been produced not long after the 1911 fall of the Ching Dynasty, at the establishment of the new Nationalist government. China's first post-dynastic national flag consisted of five differently colored horizontal stripes, each representing a different regional, racial, or religious group within China. In traditional Chinese thought, these five colors, red, yellow, blue, white, and black, were the five primary colors, each with its own set of symbolic connotations.

The Nationalist/Kuomintang flag replaced the striped flag in 1928. This new national flag had previously been in use as the Chinese naval ensign. The design was described in a 1965 Taiwan Yearbook as "White Sun in Blue Sky over Crimson Ground." Its use on the mainland ended with the 1949 Communist victory, but it is still in use in Taiwan.

Fabric label. Globe Brand. After the end of World War I, foreign business in China grew at such an alarming rate that China's emerging industrial strength was suffering a severe setback. As a result, patriotic movements started, with the purpose of promoting the sale of domestic goods and the boycotting of foreign imports. The slogans on this label read, "Promote the nation's products! Gain back profits and authority!" China, c.1920.

Fabric label. Five Children Brand. Boys engaged in a
patriotic celebration. China, 1912-1927.

Label or advertising poster. Double
Deer Brand. Tung Hsun Tang
Bleaching and Dyeing Factory.
"Promote the Nation's Products!
Gain Back Profits and Authority!"
Shantung Province, China, c.1920.

Fabric label. Pine Deer Brand. "Promote the Nation's Products! Gain Back Profits and Authority! Don't Be Deceived By Bad People Counterfeiting Our Brand!" China, 1930s.

Detail from Triple Fresh Noodles label with pre-1928 flag. Hung Cheng Shing Biscuit and Noodle Co., China, 1920s.

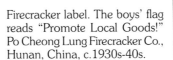

Firecracker label. The boys' flag reads "Promote Local Goods!" Po Cheong Lung Firecracker Co., Hunan, China, c.1930s-40s.

Tea tins. Tack Kee &
Co. Canton, China,
pre and post 1928.

Fabric label. Great Virtue Bleaching and
Dyeing Co. In a layout reminiscent of
traditional New Year posters, two boys
carry a giant pear, while under supervision by Lu Hsing, the god of wealth. As
usual, he carries a ru yi, the magic scepter
that fulfills the will of the beholder. The
pear was a symbol of just and able
government. Slogans on the label read,
"Promote the Nation's Products! Gain
Back Profits and Authority!" Shantung,
China, c.1920.

Fabric label. A mythical baby standing in a gold ingot holds a Nationalist flag. The baby's gleeful expression and the shining sun imply a happy, profitable future for China, while the border decorated with wheat is symbolic of a bountiful harvest. China, c. 1920s-30s.

Soap box. Essence of Rose. The national flag is crossed with a military flag.
Hua Lu Shui Soap Firm, China, c.1930.

Firecracker label. Po Sing Firecracker Factory. Three patriotic boys march under a pattern of traditional ru-yi motifs. This label was used as a shell-wrapper on large firecrackers. Nan Hai, China, c.1930.

Dye tin. Carrying Lanterns Brand. "May the Republic of China Live Ten Thousand Years." Yu Hing Dye Factory, China, c.1930.

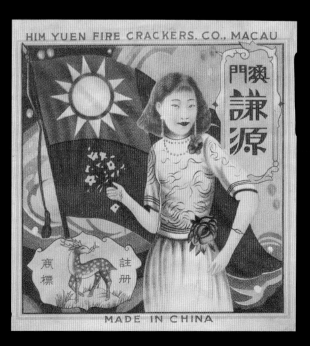

Firecracker labels. Yick Loong and Him Yuen Factories. Glamour girls demonstrate their patriotism. Several fireworks companies used this design during the era. Macau, c.1930.

Firecracker box. Globe Brand. Manufactured for the American market. Kwong Kee Chong Firecracker Co., Canton, China, c. 1930.

Firecracker label. Badger Special. Manufactured for the American market. Note the interesting interpretation of the flag's stars, also used as a border motif. Company locations in Kwangtung, Hong Kong, and Macau, 1930s.

Evolution of a Brand Design

Yan Kee Boy brand firecrackers were produced for the American market and first appeared in the early 1930s. The original design depicted two boys in traditional outfits in an affluent setting (fig. 1). While one boy crouches to light a firecracker string, the other holds the recently adopted Nationalist flag in one hand, and an American flag (with oddly triangular stars) in the other. The label's two-dimensional design in the old Chinese style is an interesting mixture of odd and impossible perspectives.

By the 1940s, the design had been reworked and now showed the two boys wearing Western clothes and haircuts (fig. 2, next page). The perspective is less two-dimensional, and the border work is more modern. The American flag has been removed and replaced with a Chinese military flag.

With the Communist government in place since 1949, many firecracker companies had closed up their branches in Canton and elsewhere, and, if possible, manufactured and exported their goods in Macau and Hong Kong. As the U.S./U.N. trade embargo with China took effect in December 1950, it became imperative to show that one's merchandise did not originate in Communist China.

By the early 1950s, the Yan Kee Boy label had been redesigned once again (fig. 3). The boy on the left now holds flags that declared no particular political allegiance, but simply read "KHT" (for Kwong Hing Tai, the manufacturer) and "Macau." The label's border has also been redesigned and is now typical of the late Art Deco influenced style still being used in the 1950s. The trademark image was redesigned, and the view is now three-dimensional, and more detailed.

An interesting feature of the new background is the inclusion of a Tibetan style pagoda (right) as well as the famed Temple of Heaven. If the Temple of Heaven is removed, the scene is an actual view of the old Winter Palace in Peking, complete with its grand entryway. The Tibetan style pagoda was built at the Winter Palace in 1652, in honor of a visit by the Dalai Lama during the previous year. It is likely that the artist's inspiration came from a photograph of the Winter Palace used on a Chinese banknote for several years beginning in 1918 (fig. 4).

The Temple of Heaven is an architectural and historical landmark located elsewhere in Peking, but was relocated by the artist for this label. Why this scene in mainland China was used during an era of tremendously strained relations between China and the U.S. is subject to debate. Perhaps it represents nostalgia for an idealized memory of old China, perhaps it was a nod to China while doing business through Macau. Or could it be nothing more than a handy scenic background?

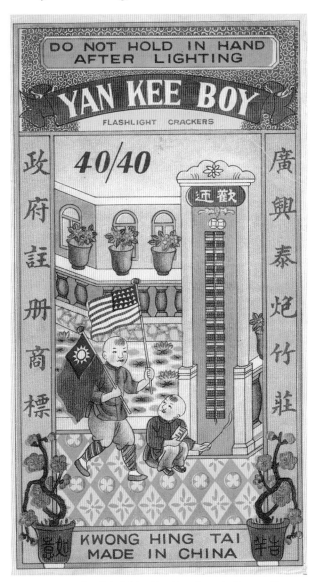

Fig. 1. Firecracker label. Yan Kee Boy Brand. Kwong Hing Tai Firecracker Co., Canton, China/ Macau, c.1930.

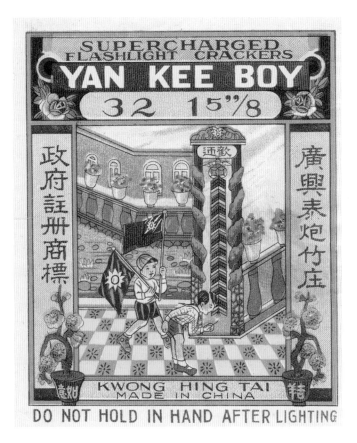

Fig. 2. Yan Kee Boy Brand. Canton, China/ Macau, c. 1940.

Fig. 3. Yan Kee Boy Brand. Macau, c.1955.

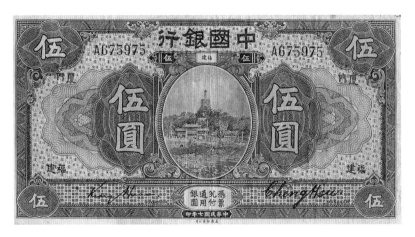

Fig. 4. Chinese banknote, 1918.

Firecracker label. Four Horsemen Brand. Warriors of old were still popular trademark subjects well into the twentieth century. Tai Hing Hong, Hong Kong, c.1940s.

Firecracker label. Chinese Warrior Brand. *Kee Chong Hong*, China, c.1935.

Firecracker label. Kwong Hing Cheong Co., China, c.1930.

Firecracker label. This warrior is Kuan Yu, a historical figure of the third century AD. His righteousness and bravery earned him the status of the god of both war and martial arts. He is also the patron god of police officers. The banner carried behind him bears Kuan's family character. China, c.1940s-50s.

Firecracker label. Tung Shun Cheong Co. On this label featuring the modern Chinese soldier of the new republic, ancient style characters are written on the vertical borders. Canton, China, c.1930.

Firecracker label. Nationalist soldier on horseback. Yick Loong Co., Macau, c.1930.

142

Candy label. China, c. 1930.

Firecracker label. Cannon trademark. Made in China for the Malaysian market. Chop Ghee Thye Co., Penang, c. 1930s-40s.

Firecracker label. Resistance Brand. Chinese Troops defend the motherland from invading Japanese forces. Kwong Wah Sing Firecracker Co., Kwangtung, China, mid-1930s.

Dried fruit box. Ho Sheng Hsiang Brand Fruit Gelatin.
"Preserved prunes-fresh, delicious national product.
Thirst-relieving prunes are necessary for marching
troops." Hong Kong, 1930s.

Cigarette pack label. Macau, c. 1930.

Cigarette pack label. Kuai Heng Tobacco Factory, Macau, 1930s.

Shirt box. Ngai Sang Knitting Factory, Hong Kong, c.1950.

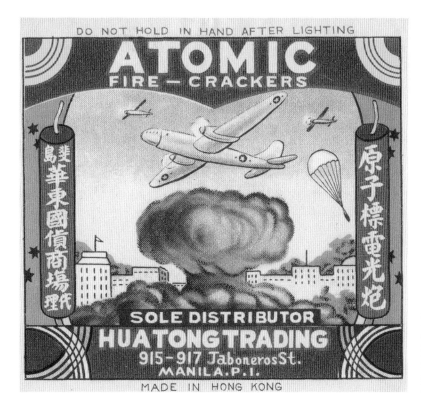

Firecracker label. Atomic Brand. Made in Hong Kong for Hua Tong Trading, Manila, Philippine Islands, c.1940s

Chapter 10
The People's Republic of China, 1949-1976

The 1949 triumph of Communism in mainland China radically altered the course of the country's advertising and packaging aesthetics. As Mao Zedong's new government disseminated its influence, an aesthetic of current political correctness began to grow within the mainland's art world. Radical changes imposed by the new government delineated clear guidelines for acceptable imagery and style in all of China's arts. Reflecting the Communist Party's ideology of stoicism and practicality, design layouts in advertising and packaging art began to loose their ornamentation and individuality.

The great advances promised by the new government were depicted in visions of a productive, technologically advanced society in which citizens were happy, healthy, prosperous, united, and under the protection of a strong army. Scenes from classic Chinese stories and legends were now frowned upon, as were the mythological beings that had been so integral to Chinese folklore. Religious iconography and symbolism became prohibited subject matter, as they represented the superstitious nature of pre-liberation China. Of no use to the revolution, these relics of old China were seen as threats to the promotion of progress and government control. The old ways of thinking were to be replaced by idealized views of a modern and prosperous China. Scenes of happy workers and modern bridges, radio towers, dams, and factories were used to instill enthusiasm for the new system, and loyalty to the new government. Ironically, the older folkloric and mythological advertising subjects, as well as the styles that had developed in the first half of the twentieth century, were still perpetuated in areas where jurisdiction was in the hands of Westerners.

A basic premise of the new Communist system was that free enterprise had to be eventually phased out. Therefore, while advertising art was still intended to help sell goods, government regulation replaced capitalist competition as the primary driving force in packaging design. State ownership would replace private ownership of business and property. The government's campaign was intended to inspire citizens to produce for the sake of national prosperity, to "serve the people," rather than to procure individual profit.

The imposed transformation did not take hold instantly. Much early-mid 1950s advertising art still reflected lingering pre-liberation remnants of the Shanghai style, on advertising and even on propaganda posters. To an extent, portrayals of beautiful women continued to be used in these early years, but women were increasingly shown actually using the product being advertised, and less as flamboyant urban sophisticates in languid scenes. Eventually, portrayals of both women and men took on standardized images of revolutionary heroes and warriors, rather than fashionable individuals with money and sex appeal.

The strictest regulations on art and advertising culminated with the Cultural Revolution (1966-1976). With the advent of Mao's last effort to fortify his political power, the eradication of beliefs regarded as superstitious and counter-revolutionary gained immense momentum. Vast numbers of old prints, books, posters, and other Chinese historical and cultural treasures were destroyed. By then, accepted style and imagery had become little more than propaganda.

Yet even under the imposition of the strictest guidelines of political ideology, interesting graphic work was produced. The best of the advertising and packaging art of the time exhibited a clean and striking design aesthetic. Despite its impersonal nature, the commercial art of this period was often carefully rendered, imaginative in its use of color, and romantic in its vision of the new, idealized utopia.

號布源利門祁

市棉運自
千萬色花

Fabric store advertising poster. Li-Yuan Fabric Store. An advertisement touting "tens of thousands of colors" of fabric portrays a China in transformation. In an illustration devoid of ornamental frills and border patterns, girls in traditional costume beat on flower drums, with happy male and female workers close behind. Confident smiles abound, against a backdrop of modern buildings, factories and towers, all symbols of progress in new China. Also present are messages of the new government's encouragement of progressive roles for women. The drummers and the female worker no longer fit the mold of the modern cosmopolitan woman, so popular in previous decades, yet their faces still echo those of the seductive beauties on the calendar posters of the past. Qi-men, PRC, early 1950s.

Advertising poster. Xun-Cheng Fabric Store. A politically charged advertisement with strong stylistic remnants of the Beautiful Woman Calendar Posters. Printed during the Korean War, it proclaims, "We welcome you to buy our flower colored fabrics. Oppose America and aid North Korea! Protect the nation and its families!" Despite the government's new aesthetic guidelines, much of the advertising work of the early to mid 1950s still reflected much of the illustrative style of pre-WW2 Shanghai. But as pointed out by Marc Riboud, author of *The Three Banners of China*, "The authorities are proud that feminine stylishness bears witness to an improvement in the standard of living, but at the same time are concerned lest it be a sign of a growing revisionist mentality." Qi-men, PRC, early 1950s.

贈敬號布成順門祁

抗美援朝
保家衛國
花色齊全
歡迎賜顧

Advertisement. White Fungus Soup and Frog Fat. From a 1958 Shanghai trade directory.

Cigarette ad. International Cigarettes. "First grade high class cigarettes." From a 1950 Shanghai City Directory.

Firecracker label. Traditional motifs were still occasionally used in the People's Republic of China during the 1950s. The butterfly and flower image, used for centuries, is an indication of fertility and happiness. Nan Hai Firecracker Factory, Nan Hai, PRC, 1950s.

Flashlight box. Shanghai, PRC, 1950s.

148

Advertising poster, medicine. New symbolism: the image of a male worker carrying a sledgehammer alongside a woman carrying a bundle of wheat became a standardized image in new China's propaganda and advertising. Here, healthy, well-dressed workers celebrate the government's image of bountiful harvests and growth in industry and commerce. Held high and also shown in the forefront is the bottle of medicine they are advertising. Kwangtung, PRC, 1950s.

Tooth powder box. PRC, 1950s.

Merchandise wrapper. Tong-Tai-Cheng sneakers and rubber shoes store. Hard work, plentiful food, military might, and equality of women are all represented on this shoe wrapper. The rounded slogan encourages the nation to be frugal and productive, in order to strengthen the country's defenses, as well as to support the People's Volunteer Army. Qing-dao, PRC, 1950s.

Firecracker label. Little Hero Brand. Nan Hai, PRC, c.1960.

Cigarette label. PRC, c.1960.

Matchbox label. For centuries, the architecture, engineering, and beauty of bridges has been of particular interest in China. As such, they have been a popular subject in art and advertising. Bridges of old were pictured as graceful, ancient monuments, usually in rural settings. After 1949, the motivation was to impress the masses with real, new bridges that glorified China's architectural and engineering marvels under Communism, and were proof of progress. PRC, late 1950s.

Matchbox label. Factory and pagoda. PRC, late 1950s.

Matchbox label. Bird and factories.
Kwangtung, PRC, 1950s.

Matchbox label. Cranes at dusk on the waterfront. PRC, late 1950s.

Matchbox label. Worker Brand. PRC, late1950s.

Matchbox label. Tiananmen Square. Sing Wha Match Co., Shanghai, PRC, 1950s.

Matchbox label. Guang Dong. Nan Hai, PRC, late 1950s.

Advertising poster for a local, government-operated brewery. Shenyan City, PRC, 1950s.

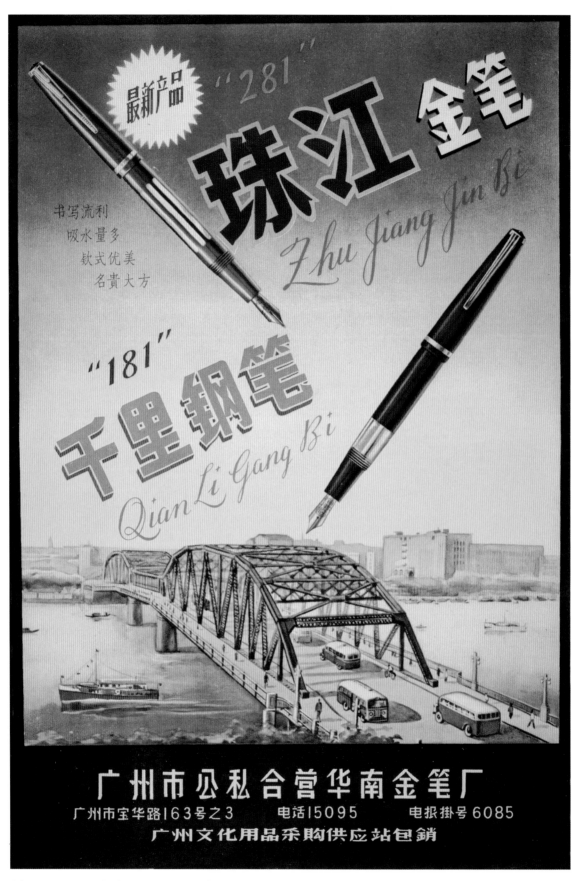

Advertising poster for fountain pens. PRC, late 1950s.

The Cultural Revolution

The Cultural Revolution began in 1966. The campaign was a result of Mao Zedong's desire to strengthen his political power, and became a movement of extremist reform and disruption that would last a decade, ending with Mao's death in 1976. In the name of progressive thinking and national security, people were encouraged to root out any signals from fellow citizens and even family members that could be construed as counter-revolutionary behavior. The discarding of old values, beliefs, loyalties, and lifestyles was central to the cause. Mao was elevated to god-like status, especially revered by the youthful Red Guards who did much of the footwork in inflicting humiliation and more serious punishments to citizens labeled as bourgeois or counterrevolutionary. With the strict regulations worked out by Mao Zedong and his wife, Jang Qing, artists, designers, actors, and musicians were to work within a narrow corridor of party-sanctioned material and style. Individual expression carried a stigma that could bring about condemnation, humiliation, imprisonment, or even death, as it had been determined that all art was to serve the masses.

Despite the turmoil and restrictive nature of the Cultural Revolution, many beautifully designed and rendered examples of advertising art were produced during this period.

Cigarette labels. PRC, late 1960s.

Fireworks label. Caizhuhua. By
the time this label came into
use, the Chinese government
had begun a campaign encour-
aging the masses to learn
phonetic spellings of Chinese
words with English letters, in an
effort to alleviate illiteracy.
PRC, c.1970.

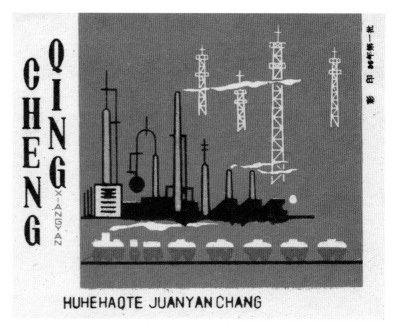

Cigarette label. Cheng Qing Brand. Highly
stylized symbols of industry.
PRC, c.1960s.

Shopping bag. Chinese native goods
store. Macau, late 1960s.

Firecracker label. Hydro-electric power plant. Nan Hai
Fireworks Factory, c. late 1960s.

156

Firecracker label. Thunder Bungers. Made in China for export to Australia. Horse Brand, China National Tea and Native Produce Import and Export Corp. Native Produce Branch, Tungoon Office, Kwangtung, c.1970.

Firecracker label. Golden Red Firecrackers. Link Triad Brand, Kwangsi, early 1970s.

Firecracker label. Tractor. From the late 1950s through the mid 1960s, production of heavy equipment greatly increased. The tractor and other machine powered farm equipment became popular subjects on everything from propaganda posters to merchandise labels, implying agricultural and industrial progress. PRC, c.1960s.

Generic masthead graphic. Revolutionary peasants encourage others to work hard and grow more crops. Achievements in agriculture and technology are attributed to study of the "little red book" of quotations from Chairman Mao. PRC, 1970.

Firecracker label. Communal farm. Stock left over from pre Cultural Revolution days had to be changed in order to meet the new graphic criteria. This label was found pasted over an earlier one depicting a peacock, from the same company. The red sun shines over a People's Commune, complete with farm machinery, a background of industry and electricity, and a bumper crop of grain. Nan Hai, PRC, c. 1966.

Merchandise label. Silver Ball Brand Ping Pong Balls. PRC, 1970s

Bibliography and Suggested Reading

Aero, Rita. *Things Chinese*. Garden City, New York: Dolphin Books, Doubleday & Company, Inc., 1980.

Ball, J. Dyer. *Things Chinese*. London: Sampson Lowe, Marston and Co., Ltd., 1888.

Berliner, Nancy Zeng. *Chinese Folk Art*. Boston, MA: Little, Brown and Company, 1986.

Bond, Ng Chun, Cheuk Pak Tong, Wong Ying, and Yvonne Lo. *Chinese Woman and Modernity: Calendar Posters of the 1910s – 1930s*. Hong Kong: Joint Publishing Co., Ltd., 1996.

Bredon, Juliet, & Igor Mitrophanow. *The Moon Year*. Shanghai: Kelly & Walsh, Limited, 1927.

Burkhardt, V. R. *Chinese Creeds and Customs. Vols. 1-3*. Hong Kong: South China Morning Post, 1955-9.

Carter, Michael. *Crafts of China*. Garden City, NY: Doubleday and Company, Inc., 1977.

China Yearbook. Taipei, Taiwan, China: China Publishing Co., 1965.

Cohen, Joan Lebold, and Jerome Alan Cohen. *China Today and Her Ancient Treasures*. New York: Harry N. Abrams, Inc., Publishers, 1975.

Coleman, Teresa. *Dragons and Silk from the Forbidden City*. Hong Kong: Odyssey Publications, Ltd., 1999.

Christie, Anthony. *Chinese Mythology*. Middlesex, England: The Hamlyn Publishing Group Limited, 1968.

Darmon, Reed. *Made in China*. San Francisco: Chronicle Books, 2004.

Eberhard. *A Dictionary of Chinese Symbols*. London and New York: Routledge & Kegan Paul, 1983.

Ecke, Tseng Yu-Ho. *Chinese Folk Art In American Collections*. New York: China Institute In America, 1976.

Go, Simon. *Hong Kong Apothecary: A Visual History of Chinese Medicine Packaging*. New York: Princeton Architectural Press, 2003.

Goodrich, L. Carrington. *A Short History of the Chinese People*. New York: Harper & Row Publishers, Inc., 1963.

Govinda, Lama Anagarika. *Psycho-cosmic Symbolism of the Buddhist Stupa*. Emeryville, CA: Dharma Press, 1976.

Hejzlar, Josef. *Early Chinese Graphics*. London: Octopus Books, 1973.

Jones, Owen. *The Grammar of Ornament*. New York: D K Publishing, Inc., 2001.

Journey Into China. Washington, DC: National Geographic Society, 1982.

Langsberger, Stefan. *Chinese Propaganda Posters*. Amsterdam and Singapore: The Pepin Press, 2005.

Leng, Seak Pau, and Guilherme Ung Vai Meng. *Pearls of Memory*. Macau: Mei Ngai Design and Publishing Co., 1999.

Ma Kam Keong, Henry. *Marcas Do Passado: Cartazes Publicitarios Chineses (1907-1953)*. Macau: Leal Senado, 1994.

Mackerass, Colin. *Modern China*. London: Thames and Hudson, Ltd., 1982.

Meggs, Philip B. *A History of Graphic Design*. New York: John Wiley & Sons, Inc., 1998.

Minick, Scott and Jiao Ping. *Chinese Graphic Design in the Twentieth Century*. London: Thames and Hudson, 1990.

Ng Chun Bong, Cheuk Pak Tong, Wong Ying, Yvonne Lo. *Chinese Woman and Modernity: Calendar Posters of the 1910s-1930s*. Hong Kong: Joint Publishing Co., Ltd., 1996.

O'Neill, Hugh B. *Companion to Chinese History*. New York and Oxford: Facts on File Publications, 1987.

Palmer, Martin, ed. *Tung Shu*. Boston, MA: Shambhala Publications, 1986.

Riboud, Marc. *The Three Banners of China*. New York: The Macmillan Company, 1966.

Roberts, Claire, ed. *Evolution & Revolution: Chinese Dress 1700s – 1900s*. Sydney: Powerhouse Publishing, 1997.

Rudova, Maria. *Chinese Popular Prints*. Leningrad: Aurora art Publishers, 1988.

Shucun, Wang. *Paper Joss*. Beijing: New World Press, 1992.

Smith, Richard J. *Chinese Almanacs.* Hong Kong: Oxford University Press, 1992.

Steep, Thomas. *Chinese Fantastics.* New York & London: The Century Co., 1925.

Stepanchuk, Carol, and Charles Wong. *Mooncakes and Hungry Ghosts: Festivals of China.* Hong Kong: China Books and Periodicals, Inc. 1991.

Szeto, Naomi Yin-yin, and Valery M. Garrett. *Children of the Gods: Dress and Symbolism In China.* Hong Kong: Urban Council, 1990.

Szeto. Naomi Yin-yin. *Dress In Hong Kong – A Century of Change and Customs.* Hong Kong: Urban Council, 1992.

Thibodeau, Michael, and Jana Martin. *Smoke gets In Your Eyes: Branding and Design in Cigarette Packaging.* New York: Abbeville Press Publishers, 2000.

Turner, Matthew. *Made in Hong Kong.* Hong Kong: Urban Council, 1990.

Williams, C. A. S. *Outlines of Chinese Symbolism and Art Motives.* New York: Dover Publications, Inc. 1976.

Williams, S. Wells, L.L.D. *The Middle Kingdom, Vol. I & II.* New York: Charles Scribner's Sons, 1907.

Yang, K. K. *Religion in Chinese Society.* Berkeley and Los Angeles, CA and London: University of California Press, 1961.

Zhensheng, Li. *Red-Color News Soldier: A Chinese Photographer's Odyssey Through The Cultural Revolution.* London & New York: Phaidon Press Limited, 2003.

Periodicals

De C. Sowerby, Arthur. "The Question of Exchange." *China Journal.* Vol. XIV, No. 5, May, 1931. Published by the North-China Daily News and Herald, Ltd. Shanghai, China.

Enns, John H. "Chinese Fireworks Labels." *Arts Of Asia.* Jan.-Feb. 1981. Arts of Asia Publications, Kowloon, Hong Kong

Richardson, H.K. "Face To Face With Business In Szechuan." *Asia Magazine.* Vol. XX, No. 4, May, 1920. Asia Publishing Co., NYC, NY.

Trade Directory: *Manufacturers of Hong Kong and South China 1937.* Mercantile Printing Press Co., Ltd., Hong Kong.

Credits

Technical advice, assistance, and image conversions: Schoonhoven Scientific Imaging Services, Durham, North Carolina. Image scanning by Andy Cahan and Robert Schoonhoven.

Images photographed by Brady Lambert:

Ch.1: pg. 14 (right); pg. 20 (bottom)

Ch.2: pg. 33 (bottom); pg. 41 (left and center); pg. 42 (bottom); pg. 47; pg. 49 (right)

Ch.3: pg. 59; pg. 61 (both right); pg. 65 (top, bottom); pg. 66 (lower right); pg. 67 (bottom)

Ch.4: pg. 72 (right, left); pg. 75 (top); pg. 77 (top); pg. 78 (center); pg. 79 (all)

Ch.5: pg. 83 (three on left); pg. 84 (bottom left, top right); pg. 85 (bottom); pg. 86 (bottom); pg. 87 (top); pg. 88 (left); pg. 89 (top left); pg. 90 (lower right); pg. 91; pg. 98 (left)

Ch.6: pg. 101 (bottom); pg. 106 (left)

Ch.7: pg. 118 (right)

Ch.8: pg. 122

Ch.10: pg. 149 (top); pg. 150 (top); pg. 153 (bottom); pg. 154; pg. 156 (bottom left)

粤東澳門

天祥

雙鳳朝陽焉記

遴庄各品名香

CHAN TIN CHUNG

MACAO

為記別人不得假冒几
士商光顧請認箱內每包
加點石小印爵祿封侯採
辦庶免有悮舖在粤東
澳門康公廟前北向開張
陳天祥主人謹識